You Might Be a
MORMON
If...

TALK TAPES BY MICHAEL ALLRED

Get Ready . . . Get Set . . . Date!
You Might Be a Mormon If . . .

You Might Be a
MORMON
If...

Michael Weir Allred

Covenant Communications, Inc.

The views of this book are mine. They do not necessarily reflect the views of Mormons in general or the official doctrines of The Church of Jesus Christ of Latter-day Saints.

Where quoted material is used, the complete reference is given at the end of this book in the Selected Bibliography.

Chapter Eight, "You Might Be a Mormon If . . . The Spirit Is Your Image Consultant" originally appeared in *Return with Honor, Favorite Talks from Especially for Youth,* published by Bookcraft, Salt Lake City,Utah,1995, under the title of "You Tell on Yourself: What You Are Inside Will Show Up Outside." It is reprinted here with permission.

Chapter Two, "You Might Be a Mormon If . . . You Treasure the Power of Truth," originally appeared in *Treasure the Truth, Favorite Talks from Especially for Youth, Academy for Girls, and Boys World of Adventure,* published by Covenant Communications, Inc., American Fork, Utah,1997, under the title of "The Power of Truth: How to Resist, Regroup, and Respond to Temptation." It is also reprinted here with permission.

Published by Covenant Communications, Inc.
American Fork, Utah

Printed in the United States of America
First Printing: June 1998

05 04 03 02 01 00 99 98   10 9 8 7 6 5 4 3 2 1

ISBN 1-57734-285-2

CONTENTS

I would like to recognize my friends at Covenant for the motivation, encouragement, and support to write this book.

And a special thanks to those who helped me by reading and listening to my ideas—Lynn and Ed Eyestone, Valoy Scott, Brooklyn Robins, Pen Bradshaw, and Shelley Dockstader.

To my very best friend, companion, and wife, Kathy. Thanks for making it fun and easy to be a husband.

To my four sons—Tyson, Joshua, Cody, and Kade. Arise, go forth, and conquer!

To my heroes—Dad, you taught me how to laugh. Mom, you taught me how to love.

In my mind, teaching is not merely a life work, a profession, an occupation, a struggle; it is a passion. I love to teach.

I love to teach as a painter loves to paint, as a musician loves to play, as a singer loves to sing, as a strong man rejoices to run a race. . . .

William Lyon Phelps

INTRODUCTION

Have you ever considered how different we, as Mormons, are? That there is something unique about us? Not only do we have our own "special" vocabulary, but we think a little differently, too. In 1993, while I was preparing an introduction for a talk about standing up for righteousness, I was considering the advantages of this distinctiveness and how I might introduce it. Then it hit me, like the popular comedian who talks about distinguishing "rednecks," we might also be able to identify Mormons. With the help of some of my students we determined "You might be a Mormon if . . ."

- Your family reunion involves a whole city.
- You're in a beauty pageant's swimsuit contest and you have to wear a T-shirt.
- "Party on" means Twister, G-movies, and S'mores.
  You think green Jell-O salad is a major food group.
  Your family drives into a small town and doubles the population.
- When you buy a prom dress, you need another yard of material to cover it up.
- Your favorite phrase is "Oh my heck."
- You had a party and someone spiked the punch with Pepsi.
- Your dad cheated to win the Pinewood Derby.

As we can see, Mormons are a peculiar people (see 1 Peter 2:9). And rightly so. The Lord needs us to stand up and be noticed. Maybe not by some of these amusing ways, but by the way we live the gospel of Jesus Christ in our daily lives.

In the mid-80s, I began training as a counter intelligence agent in the Utah Army National Guard. I really enjoyed the training, but I never did any "real world" spying. At the time, the active duty evaluators were a little concerned about returned missionaries with language skills trying to become spies. Not that our language abilities were deficient or that we couldn't be trusted with secret information, but we did not blend into the environment in which spying usually takes place. For example, let me share an eventful training experience. First, it is helpful for you to know that there are two different kinds of surveillance: *close* and *discreet*. Both have their priority. In a close surveillance, you stay with the person (known as "the rabbit") even if he knows someone is on him. In a discreet surveillance, it is imperative that the rabbit not know he is being followed. On one occasion, while on a close surveillance, I rotated to what is sometimes called the "A" position. This means that in the team of agents I was working with, I had the responsibility of staying close. The other three agents would continue watching the rabbit while keeping an eye on me for hand signals (similar to baseball signals). If the rabbit were to walk into a building I would stay on him.

I think the evaluator, who was also acting as the rabbit, wanted to see what my limits were. What would a Mormon returned missionary do in a worldly situation? He went into a bookstore and I followed him. He knew what he was doing. He stood in such a way that I had no option to go anywhere else in the store but one area. The PORNO section. As I glanced at the book covers, I was a little nervous. I did not want to pick one up. But my job as a spy was to blend into the environment that I was in. I knew I was running out of time; I had to think and act fast. I could not afford to stick out and be noticed. So I reached across the top of the section that I was in and grabbed a book—*any* book—from the other side. I didn't care what it was. I just needed to appear to be looking and reading something while keeping my eye on the rabbit.

I didn't totally fail in this challenge. I *almost* blended in. I was looking at a book like the other men in that section of the store. However, the book I had grabbed from the "normal section" was, to my amusement, a cookbook. I was the only man in the porno area scanning through different ways to prepare a casserole!

It felt really odd for me, as a Mormon spy-to-be, to walk into a bar and say, "I'll have a root beer please." But that is who we are. We stand out.

During another surveillance, that same rabbit walked into a Triple-X theater. It happened at a time when I had just rotated to the "A" position again. Not only did I look out of place in the ticket line, but because I could not see the rabbit anywhere in the lobby, I said to the man at the counter, "Excuse me sir, may I use your restroom?" The words came naturally to me, but can you imagine anyone in that type of place saying, "Excuse me sir, may I . . . ?" I don't think so. Luckily the evaluator had gone out the back door and sounded the emergency escape alarm so I did not have to spend my money and actually go into the theater after all.

As you can see from these experiences, we are a peculiar people. We are in the world, but the scriptures teach us not to be "of the world" (see John 17:15-16). Nevertheless, the Lord needs us to be identified. Missionary work is on its way when someone notices us for our unique behavior and asks, "Are you a Mormon or something?" Now we have the opportunity to teach.

You Might Be a Mormon If . . . is about identifying and celebrating the distinguishing advantages of being a Mormon.

Chapter One

You Stand Up for Righteousness

In spring general conference of 1992, President Gordon B. Hinckley said:

> Some time ago, I read a letter to a newspaper editor which was highly critical of the Church. I have forgotten the exact language, but it included a question something like this: When are the Mormons going to stop being different and become a part of mainstream America?
>
> About this same time there came to my desk a copy of an address given by Senator Dan Coats of Indiana. He spoke of a study made by "a commission of educational, political, medical and business leaders" dealing with problems of American youth. . . .
>
> Suicide is now the second leading cause of death among adolescents. . . .
>
> More than a million teenage girls get pregnant each year.
>
> Eighty-five percent of teenage boys who impregnate teenage girls eventually abandon them.
>
> Homicide is now the leading cause of death among fifteen- to nineteen-year-old minority youth. . . .
>
> A third of high school seniors get drunk once a week.

The average age for first-time drug use is now thirteen years old. *(Imprimis,* September 1991, p. 1)

When I read those statements, I said to myself, If that is the mainstream of American youth, then I want to do all in my power to persuade and encourage our young people to stay away from it. (*Conference Report,* April 1992, pp. 96-97)

As Latter-day Saints we also have problems, and all is not well in Zion, but something is working. Our youth seem to be able to avoid some of the negative influences of the world. But by the very manner with which they avoid these influences, they are thought of as being different, as "goody-goody." One of the worst insults you can give Mormon youth is to call them a Molly Mormon. The worldly do not want to have others stand out as being better or more righteous than they are. Go ahead, call me a Molly Mormon, a Peter Priesthood, a Rachel Relief Society. I like the compliment. Is it bad to be thought of as being Christlike?

The Lord needs us to stand up and be noticed for being good. Not that we do our alms before the world to be seen of the world (see Matthew 6:1), but that we become a living testimony of Jesus Christ in all areas of our lives, following Him with our "head, shoulders, knees and toes," as well as our "eyes, ears, mouth and nose" *(Children's Songbook,* p. 25).

HEAD - *Before you can stand you have to think.*

From several of the Civil War era movies we see that the greatest place of honor was to be the flag holder, or what is better called the "standard bearer." This is the one who holds up the standard for all to see, even as the battle intensifies, so that all may rally around and defend its symbolically implied purpose. Captain Moroni was not only the leader of the Nephite armies, but he was also their first standard bearer. Remember how in Alma chapter 46, he took his coat and wrote their pledge upon it, then held it up high for others to rally around? He was not ashamed of the principles he believed in, but rather he was courageous as he invited others to join him. We should not be ashamed of anything we believe in, but we should stand tall and invite others to join us.

Have you heard that saying which says, "When in Rome do as the Romans do?" Have you also heard the scripture in Romans that reads, "I am ready to preach the gospel to you that are at Rome also. For I am not ashamed of the gospel of Christ; for it is the power of God unto salvation. . . ." (Romans 1:15-16). The Apostle Paul was willing to preach to the Romans, not conform to them. When others are following Christ, it is okay to do as they are doing, but only when it agrees with the Savior's standards. Elder Neal A. Maxwell said it this way:

> Even while bravely following correct principles, we should meekly strive to make those correct principles popular rather than ourselves. . . . There is no way we can both move with the herd and also move toward Jesus. . . . We cannot improve the world if we are conformed to the world (see Romans 12:2). The gospel represents constancy amid change, not compliant adaptation to changing fashions and trends. Firm followers of Jesus, therefore, will not be mere chameleons—adapting their colors to match the ever-changing circumstances by simply blending in. (*Ensign*, March 1995, p. 15)

SHOULDERS - Stand *on your own shoulders.*

Even though I spent most of my part-time military career in the Army National Guard, I started off in the Air Force Reserves. This chapter of my life began after I had already served a full-time mission. The first Sunday at Lackland Air Force Base, in Texas, we were given the choice of attending either Catholic or Protestant services. Our military leaders wanted to keep everybody together as much as possible so they did not give us any other options. The next week, however, we could attend our own denominational services. Knowing this, I stood up and invited everyone to go to the LDS church with me next week. The others already knew I was a Mormon because my underwear was just a little bit different from theirs. The first Sunday that we were allowed to attend the church of our choice, several of the other men joined me. Before our six-week basic training was over, I had the wonderful opportunity of baptizing one of them. And every night all fifty of us would gather around my bunk and we would have family prayer. It wasn't my idea, but for some reason the others always wanted me to say it.

We need to raise our standards for the world to see and invite everyone to come unto Christ. In Psalms we read, "I will speak of thy testimonies also before kings, and will not be ashamed" (Psalm 119:46). With this responsibility placed upon us, we cannot afford to be afraid. John A. Widstoe said:

> We need, in this Church and Kingdom, for our own and the world's welfare a group of men and women in their individual lives who shall be as a light to the nations, and rally standards for the world to follow. Such a people must be different from the world as it now is. There is no opportunity for Latter-day Saints to say we shall be as the world is, unless the world has the same aim that we have. We are here to build Zion to Almighty God, for the blessing of all the world. In that aim we are unique and different from all other peoples. We must respect that obligation, and not be afraid of it. We cannot walk as other men, or talk as other men, or do as other men, for we have a different destiny, obligation, and responsibility placed upon us, and we must fit ourselves for that great destiny and obligation. *(Conference Report,* April 5, 1940, p. 36)

KNEES - *Before you can stand, you have to kneel.*

President Spencer W. Kimball taught us that the passport to spiritual power is prayer (see *Ensign,* July 1973, p.17). Prayer becomes the beginning of the confidence we need to stand up for what we believe in. In an article published in the *Church News,* President Kimball wrote what appears as a want ad for our LDS youth entitled "Youth Leaders Wanted." It read:

> **Wanted:** Youth who will listen to counsel of those who have lived life and who know the joys of [obedience] and the sorrows of disobedience.
>
> **Wanted:** Youth who live their lives [unchained] by the faddish fads, uninfluenced by the idiosyncrasies of the oddballs and the [weird] would-be leaders.
>
> **Wanted:** Young folks who will not, like sheep, jump over the cliff merely because the whole band before them have leaped to their destruction below; but youth who stand "by their guns" yielding only to those social and crowd pressures which wisdom labels proper.
>
> **Wanted:** Youth who will resist all anti-social influences [against] proper development; youth who will lead in proper dance patterns and foster group activities for many of the teenage years.
>
> **Wanted:** Youth who will be the masters rather than slaves of styles [and] customs, . . . bright youth who will maintain a middle-of-the-road course in modest make-up, hairdos, dress, talk, dance, and dates, avoiding the [chains] of the radical extremes.
>
> **Wanted:** Youth, who though outnumbered in the group, dare to stand firm for [principles of righteousness] even through criticism or taunting. . . .
>
> **Wanted:** A young generation who will yield to no unrighteous pressures, surrender to no cheap prac-

tices, submit to no immoral activities. Youth who will die before sacrificing honor and virtue. *(Church News,* 13 February 1960, pp. 4, 7)

Wow, what a great list! Can you imagine what a better place this world would be if all youth would answer this want ad? We need to spend a lot of time on our knees to receive this level of spiritual power through prayer.

Many of us cannot see ourselves making such a strong stand. Occasionally we don't even understand why we are required to live a certain way, and at times some standards don't make sense. But that is the time to follow the counsel of the familiar scripture Joshua 24:15, which reads, "And if it seem evil unto you to serve the Lord, choose you this day whom ye will serve . . . but as for me and my house, we will serve the Lord." Even when it seems wrong, stupid, or old fashioned, it is time to choose to serve the Lord. Now is the time to decide to make a stand. The Lord will help. All we need to do is ask in faith.

TOES - *As you stand, don't step on anyone's toes.*

Before I left on my mission, I spent a year working in Indianapolis trying to save some money. The office I worked in was a drafting room for the city planning department. Since I was the only Mormon in the room, the other four employees frequently asked questions about my beliefs and I was able to hand out a few Book of Mormons. Not only did I enjoy teaching them about the gospel, but I always tried to do and say things that would create doctrinal conversations.

On one occasion after work, I went to a bank's automatic teller machine to withdraw some of my savings. The machine gave me too much money. At first I was excited about receiving extra cash, but then it dawned on me that it was not mine. How could I keep it when it wasn't mine? But, I asked myself, was it the bank's? The next day at work, I made a phone call using the office telephone. I said, "Hi. Yesterday I pulled some money out of my account and the machine gave me too much. If you can tell me how much it was, so I know it's yours, I'll bring it back." I gave them my work number and hung up. Everyone in the office heard the conversation. Some listened in disbelief. My supervisor said, "That was the stupidest thing I've ever heard. Do you know how much that bank takes from you in interest. You should just put that money in your pocket and be glad you got it."

Soon after, the bank called back and reported the proper amount that I had received. So after work I took the money and gave it back to the bank. The guys at work really harassed me about it, but I think they trusted me after that. I don't think my boss was worried about me stealing pencils from work. From this I learned that it is imperative we set a proper example to our nonmember friends. By the way, one of my co-workers was later baptized.

Sometimes our conduct becomes a roadblock to others entering the strait and narrow path. Alma charged his wayward son, Corianton, to repent and told him of the difficulties he was creating for the work of God. He said, "O my son, how great iniquity ye brought upon the Zoramites; for when they saw your conduct they would not believe in my words" (Alma 39:11). One man's conduct hampered the missionaries' efforts. We cannot afford to set a bad example. We have to stay strong and true. Remember, you may be the only scriptures your friends ever read.

EYES - *Keep your eyes single to His glory.*

Just how much effect does what we see have over us? I'm always curious to hear the results of studies on this matter. When I was about fourteen years old, my sixteen-year-old brother showed me how a 30-30 lever action rifle worked. It was the kind of rifle I used to see in an old show called *The Rifleman*. He showed me how seven shells slipped into the side, then as fast as he could, he swung the lever down, then up again, forcing all the bullets to fly out of the top without being fired. (The gun wouldn't shoot unless the trigger was pulled.)

He loaded the gun again and again, each time improving the speed with which he could eject the shells. It was fun to watch. My five-year-old nephew and I were amazed.

When we were finished, my brother put the rifle back in the gun cabinet and set the bullet belt on top of the cabinet. Because he was still working on the cabinet, it could not be locked. In fact, it didn't even have a door.

Later that evening, my brother and I invited a friend over so we could play some music. My brother played guitar, I played the drums, and our friend played the piano. My extremely supportive mom sat and listened with joy. (Not that we were any good, but that was just my mom.) My nephew wanted to participate, so I told him to go in the closet by the gun cabinet and get the bongo drums. He was gone a little while, and I forgot all about him. As we played and my mom smiled, I heard a very loud "boom!" I knew that boom did not come from my bass drum. I stopped playing for a second and said, "It sounded like a car just hit the house." Everyone laughed and assured me that a car had not hit the house, and we continued to play. My nephew came back to join us, but he didn't bring the bongo drums so I assumed he couldn't find them.

When the evening of music was over, our friend went home and I went into my bedroom to go to sleep. To my surprise, my bed was made. I hate to admit it, but making my bed was not one of my teenage habits. As I pulled down the covers, I noticed that my sheets were ripped, and there was black powder on them. And for some unknown reason the shade of my lamp was all bent up. I thought it was strange, but I was young and tired and started to get into bed. The mattress compressed under my weight, and I noticed a hole in the wall right below the surface level of my bed.

"Mom!" I yelled. "Someone shot a bullet into our house." She ran in and we inspected the hole. We immediately called the police, and as we waited, we wondered where that bullet could have come from. Remembering my boyish duty, I began to tease my nephew, "The police are coming to get ya, the police are coming to get ya." He started to cry a little and whine, "They are not!" Because of his reaction I kept teasing him. You see, like most boys that age, I fully understood that my responsibility in life was to annoy people.

When the policeman arrived, he asked us several questions, then asked us to follow him outside. With his flashlight, he peered into the hole in the siding on our house. Then he said confidently, "Ma'am, this bullet came from *inside* the house." We asked how he determined that.

"There is mattress material in your wall," he answered.

We returned to the house and examined the facts. The rifle was sitting in its spot in the gun cabinet but the action was left wide open. Set upright next to the rifle was an empty cartridge. This is what had happened. My five-year-old nephew had gone into my bedroom to get the bongos. As he opened the closet, the door had bumped the gun belt on top of the cabinet, knocking out a cartridge. This little boy had seen so many times how to load the rifle, that he took the shell, slid it in, opened the action, and placed the bullet in the chamber. When he sat the rifle down on my bed, it went off.

A five-year-old using a 30-30 rifle? He had seen it done so many times that it was easy for him. What really amazed me is that he put the rifle away and neatly made my bed. Now that is amazing. A five-year-old making a bed!

Just like my nephew, we remember things that we see. Satan is very clever at deceiving people, and he understands very well how to use the media to teach us his ways. Popular movies and even magazines provide an endless list of examples. President Kimball described some of the tools and tactics Satan uses to deceive us.

- He uses logic to confuse. ("Mom, I know it's rated R, but I hear worse language at school.")
- He uses rationalization to destroy. ("There is only one bad part.")

- He shades meanings. ("I don't know why my bishop said it was a bad show. I thought it was pretty good.")
- He opens the door an inch at a time. ("There's really not much difference between a PG-13 and R, so we might as well see the R show.")
- He leads from the purest white through all the shades of gray to the darkest black. ("It was such a beautiful love story, and the man and the woman really loved each other, so it was okay.") (See Spencer W. Kimball, *Ensign,* November 80, p. 94.)

EARS - *Listen to whom you stand with.*

A popular rock band was scheduled to give a concert in Salt Lake City. The warm-up band they were on tour with were told by the city they could not play in Salt Lake. During the concert, one of the members of the band that was not allowed to play came out on stage and held up a Book of Mormon. He mentioned to the crowd that the Book of Mormon was controlling too many of their lives, then he preceded to rip it apart on stage. The audience went crazy cheering. One of my seminary students was in the audience and told me it gave him a very sick feeling to hear people cheering for such a thing. Another young man I met from Colorado said that those same two bands were in concert together in Denver. He said that all through the concert they kept "bad mouthing" the Mormons. Does this conduct surprise anyone?

In the very book ripped up by the band member, the Book of Mormon, there is a scripture that reads:

> Wherefore, he that fighteth against Zion, both Jew and Gentile, both bond and free, both male and female, shall perish; for they are they who are the whore of all the earth; for they who are not for me are against me, saith our God. (2 Nephi 10:16)

Was the band on stage for the Lord or against the Lord? It should not be difficult to understand who we should make our stand with. The Lord needs us on His side. We need to be on His side. No one has to tell us who the band was or which bands we should listen to. Just remember the previous scripture and ask, "Are they for the Lord or against the Lord?" Then choose you this day with whom you will stand.

MOUTH - *Stand by your words.*

One of the biggest complaints we hear from young women concerns those Aaronic Priesthood holders who bless the sacrament on Sunday, but use vulgar language throughout the week. This should never occur. We cannot serve two masters (see Matthew 6:24). From the third chapter of the Epistle of James we are taught:

> My brethren, be not many masters, knowing that we shall receive the greater condemnation.
>
> For in many things we offend all. If any man offend not in word, the same is a perfect man, and able also to bridle the whole body.
>
> Behold, we put bits in the horses' mouths, that they may obey us; and we turn about their whole body.
>
> Behold also the ships, which though they be so great, and are driven of fierce winds, yet are they turned about with a very small helm, whithersoever the governor listeth.
>
> Even so the tongue is a little member, and boasteth great things. Behold, how great a matter a little fire kindleth!
>
> And the tongue is a fire, a world of iniquity: so is the tongue among our members, that it defileth the whole body, and setteth on fire the course of nature; and it is set on fire of hell.

For every kind of beasts, and of birds, and of serpents, and of things in the sea, is tamed, and hath been tamed of mankind:

But the tongue can no man tame; it is an unruly evil, full of deadly poison. Therewith bless we God, even the Father; and therewith curse we men, which are made after the similitude of God.

Out of the same mouth proceedeth blessing and cursing. My brethren, these things ought not so to be.

Doth a fountain send forth at the same place sweet water and bitter?

Can the fig tree, my brethren, bear olive berries? either a vine, figs? so can no fountain both yield salt water and fresh.

Who is a wise man and endued with knowledge among you? Let him shew out of a good conversation his works with meekness of wisdom. (James 3:1-13)

We must show good conversation so that others may know who our master is. Swearing is not new or original; it is just plain wrong. It sets a bad example for others and develops the wrong impression of what we stand for.

NOSE - *It's your nose; stand up for it.*

You may have thought I was going to warn you to be careful of the things you smell but I am not. Have you ever seen a bull being led around by a large ring in his nose? President Kimball had that responsibility when he was young. He said that if the bull got out of hand, he would yank on the chain connected to the ring in its nose, and the bull would immediately become submissive. As Latter-day Saints, we must not let anyone lead us about by our noses. We were not sent to this earth to be led by the nose, we were sent here to be missionaries by example for Jesus Christ. In his book *Gospel Doctrine*, Joseph F. Smith said, "The people of Zion have a higher destiny than being led by the nose, as it were, by the prevailing whims. We do not purpose being led by evil tendencies, but rather glory in being leaders ourselves. . . ." (p. 305).

In other words, we cannot allow ourselves to submit to the world's morals. Richard L. Evans said:

> Evil will go just as far as we let it. If we patronize it, encourage it, it will go to unlimited lengths. But we personally can play an important part by not patronizing, not purchasing, not making profitable anything of evil or of low-minded morals. If something isn't good for people, it doesn't matter how profitable or popular or prevalent it is, we ought to leave it alone. (Richard L. Evans, *Thoughts*, p. 128)

When the world has new R-rated movies, we follow the prophet. When the world changes swimsuits, we stay with our standards. When the world calls it normal, we stand up for right.

CONCLUSION

Our focus and determination should be to stand up for righteousness and to be noticed for being a Mormon. President Benson taught, "Each day the forces of evil and the forces of good pick up new recruits. Each day we personally make many decisions that show where our support will go. The final outcome is certain—the forces of righteousness will finally win. What remains to be seen is where each of us personally, now and in the future, will stand in this fight—and how tall we will stand" (BYU 14-Stake Fireside, 4 March 1979).

The scriptures tell us to be an example of a believer in word, conversation, charity, spirit, faith, and purity (see 1 Timothy 3:12). Even outside the Church we are advised:

> Submit to pressure from peers and you move down to their level. Speak up for your own beliefs

and you invite them up to your level. If you move with the crowd, you'll get no further than the crowd. When 40 million people believe in a dumb idea, it's still a dumb idea. Simply swimming with the tide leaves you nowhere. So if you believe in something that's good, honest and bright—stand up for it. Maybe your peers will get smart and drift your way. ("Will the Real You Please Stand Up?" Sigma Chi Fraternity, *Literary Exercises*, Copyright 1995-1997; available at http://is2.dal.ca/~rlidston/le.html [1998 Apr 27].)

Now is the time to invite others to join us. We need to hold up our standards so others can rally around. Our lives will become our testimonies as we help others come unto Christ. President Gordon B. Hinckley, in one of his first speeches as prophet and president of the Church, said,

> The time has come for us to stand a little taller. . . . This is a season to be strong. It is a time to move forward without hesitation. . . . It is a time to do what is right regardless of the consequences that might follow. It is a time to be found keeping the commandments. It is a season to reach out with kindness and love to those in distress and to those who are wandering in darkness and pain. It is a time to be considerate and good, decent and courteous toward one another in all our relationships. In other words, to become more Christlike. (*Ensign*, May 1995, p. 71)

Chapter Two

You Treasure the Power of Truth

Dear Jim,

Last night you pleaded with me to prove my love for you. You said that when two people really love each other as much as we do, it's only natural to share that love completely. You were very persuasive. And because of the deep feelings I have for you, it was hard to deny you. For hours after I left I was afraid of losing you. Afraid that I had made a terrible mistake. But today I'm thankful from the depths of my heart that I did not give in to you. I am so relieved that I don't have to bear the terrible burden of having lost my virtue. In the middle of the night I got up and opened the Book of Mormon to a verse that I had somehow remembered, where Mormon is writing to his son Moroni. I could really feel his horror and sorrow as he told of the terrible cruelty of the Nephite soldiers to the Lamanite maidens. Many of the daughters of the Lamanites had been taken prisoner, he said, and deprived of "that which is most dear and precious above all things, which is chastity and virtue." These words of Mormon, "that which is most dear and precious above all things, which is chastity and virtue", came powerfully into my mind last night. I read them over and over again.

I wonder if I could help you understand just a little what you were asking. You are so proud of your new car. What would you say if someone asked you to give up your car as proof of your affection for her. You would think she was joking. If she persisted, you might question her motive or her sincerity. Yet you could get another car.

But how could either of us ever know if we would be willing to pay the price, the terrible cost of restoring virtue—yours as well as mine. Last night you asked me to surrender my purity and self-respect for a few minutes of excitement and pleasure for yourself. Your talk of my proving my love for you was a bitter mockery. If you really love me, you'll have to prove to me that virtue means more to you than pleasure. That you think more of us than you do of yourself.

Elizabeth

(Hold to the Rod, Scripture Motivation and Comprehension Series, Video Presentation 1, "Hold to the Rod," Church Educational System, 1984)

This letter reflects a common problem. How many times has Satan influenced someone to use the phrase, "If you love me . . ." In fact, it is so common, why would anyone fall for it? How come so many are deceived into believing that this is love? But what about Elizabeth? She was able to resist, regroup, and respond to the pressures of her boyfriend. Where did her strength come from?

As we analyze the narrative, we see that she was strong enough to resist. That resistance bought her some time. During the time that she was alone, thinking about what had just happened, Satan did not stop tempting her. Had she just lost her boyfriend? Would he still love her? Did he really love her in the first place? Had she made the right decision? These kind of questions lay heavy on her mind, making it a sleepless night.

Finally, because of her righteousness, the Spirit prompted her and a scripture came into her mind. She opened her Book of Mormon to the inspired scripture and was strengthened by an understanding of a true doctrine. She gained power through knowing that chastity and virtue is most dear and precious above all things. And having received this answer from the Lord, there was no way that the gates of hell were going to prevail against her. She was able to regroup with the Spirit, getting back to where she needed to be.

Jim had been deceived. Elizabeth discovered the lies and was able to find the truth. She now knew the truth about the value of chastity. She knew the truth about Jim, too—that he was only thinking of himself. No wonder the scriptures teach us to gird our loins with truth (Ephesians 6:14). When we know the truth, we can see that where there is temptation, there is a lie. Think about it. With truth the phrase would be, "If you love me, if you truly love me, you will want what is best for me—chastity, virtue, and eternal life." The power is in the truth. Elizabeth was able to respond to Jim in a way that might help him to resist the temptations he was feeling and regroup with the Spirit, which he needed so desperately.

Here are three recommendations for receiving eternal truth. They are *preparation*, *pursuit*, and *power*.

PREPARATION - *The process of making ready for use*

The first step in obtaining truth is to prepare for the truth. Before you can eat a nut, you have to crack the hard shell on the outside. If we are not spiritually prepared, we will not understand spiritual truths. For the natural man thinks that spiritual things are foolishness (see 1 Corinthians 2:14). What good would it do if Heavenly Father gave us spiritual insight before we were ready to receive it? It would be like a dad giving his two-year-old the keys to the family car!

Here are four elements of preparation required before receiving truth from the Spirit: *Desire, Faith, Repentance,* and *Obedience*.

Desire	But behold, if ye will awake and arouse your faculties, even to an experiment upon my words, and exercise a particle of faith, yea even if ye can no more than *desire* to believe, let this *desire* work in you, even until ye believe in a manner that ye can give place for a portion of my words. (Alma 32:27; empashis added)

Humility   And inasmuch as they were humble
                  they might be made strong, and blessed
                  from on high, and receive knowledge
                  from time to time. (D&C 1:28)

Faith   And in that day that they shall exercise
                  faith in me, saith the Lord, even as the
                  brother of Jared did . . . then will I
                  manifest unto them the things which
                  the brother of Jared saw, even to the
                  unfolding unto them all my revela-
                  tions. . . . (Ether 4:7)

Repentance   And now behold, my brethren, what
                  natural man is there that knoweth these
                  things? I say unto you, there is none
                  that knoweth these things, save it be the
                  penitent. (Alma 26:21)

Obedience   If any man will do his will, he shall
                  know of the doctrine, whether it be of
                  God, or whether I speak of myself.
                  (John 7:17)

As we prepare ourselves for the truth, we become attuned to spiritual things. We are now ready to learn from the Spirit.

PURSUIT - *To work to obtain*

Once we have prepared ourselves we need to seek the truth. We need not suppose that the Lord will just give it to us; we need to do our part (see D&C 9:7-8).

Consider the Missionary Training Center. Why doesn't the Lord just give us foreign language ability and ship us out to the mission field? Why do we have to memorize scriptures? Why doesn't he just put the quotes into our brains? While on my mission, I remember hearing a quote that said, "Together you and the Lord can move mountains, but don't be surprised if He hands you the shovel." Sometimes receiving truth from the Spirit might seem like moving a mountain to get a treasure, but it is a mountain He wants us to move. He wants us to have that treasure.

Here are five suggestions for obtaining truth: *Study, Ponder, Pray, Fast,* and *Apply.*

> **Study**   Search the scriptures; for in them ye think ye have eternal life: and they are they which testify of me. (John 5:39)

President Ezra Taft Benson stressed the importance of studying the gospel when he said, "We should make daily study of the scriptures a lifetime pursuit. . . . The most important [thing] you can do . . . is to immerse yourselves in the scriptures. Search them diligently. . . . Learn the doctrine" *(Ensign,* November 1986, p. 47).

> **Ponder**   This book of the law shall not depart out of thy mouth; but thou shalt meditate therein day and night, that thou mayest observe to do according to all that is written therein: for then thou shalt make thy way prosperous, and then thou shalt have good success. (Joshua 1:8)

We need to understand that "the things of God are of vast importance, and require time and experience as well as deep and solemn thought to find them out" (from a letter written by Joseph Smith, Hyrum Smith, and Lyman Wight while in prison, printed in *The Times and Seasons*, vol. 4, no. 7, May 1840; reprinted in *Teachings of the Latter-day Prophets,* pp. 341-42).

Pray	If any of you lack wisdom, let him ask of God, that giveth to all men liberally, and upbraideth not; and it shall be given him. (James 1:5)

Joseph Smith said, "The best way to obtain truth and wisdom is not to ask it from books, but to go to God in prayer and obtain divine teaching" (*Teachings of the Prophet Joseph Smith*, p. 191).

Fast	Behold, I say unto you they are made known unto me by the Holy Spirit of God. Behold, I have fasted and prayed many days that I might know these things of myself. And now I do know of myself that they are true; for the Lord God hath made them manifest unto me by his Holy Spirit; and this is the spirit of revelation which is in me. (Alma 5:46)

Apply	Therefore whosoever heareth these sayings of mine, and *doeth* them, I will liken him unto a wise man, which built his house upon a rock (Matthew 7:24; emphasis added).

As we seek the truth by studying, pondering, fasting, praying, and applying the truth in our lives, we open a treasure that lasts forever. The more we find, the more there is, until we have all that our Father in Heaven has. That is the way He wants it.

POWER - *Strength to act, produce, and perform*

There are many examples of how we can receive the truth (see Matthew 7:16). One of the fruits of truth is power. Have you ever considered that there are many things we plug into electrical power? The power is the same, but the application depends on what is plugged in. So it is with truth. The Spirit blesses us with truth, which gives us the strength to act, produce, and perform. Notice that this power shows up in various areas of our lives:

Power to Resist:
The desire for sin

> . . . the nearer man approaches perfection, the clearer are his views, and the greater his enjoyments, till he has overcome the evils of his life and lost every desire for sin. . . . *(Teachings of the Prophet Joseph Smith,* p. 51)

The gates of hell

> Then said Jesus to those Jews which believed on him, If ye continue in my word, then are ye my disciples indeed; And ye shall know the truth, and the truth shall make you free. (John 8:31-32)

President Harold B. Lee taught that "truth is the scepter of power, which if man possesses, will give him 'dominion' and the ability to 'subdue all things'" *(Teachings of the Latter-day Prophets,* p. 188). This power is so vital that we should not fail to obtain it. President Joseph F. Smith said, "The greatest achievement mankind can make in this world is to familiarize themselves with divine truth, so thoroughly, so perfectly, that the example or conduct of no creature living in the world can ever turn them away from the knowledge that they have obtained" *(Gospel Doctrine,* pp. 3-4). And listen to the words of Helaman to his sons:

> And now, my sons, remember, remember that it is upon the rock of our Redeemer, who is Christ, the Son of God, that ye must build your foundation;

that when the devil shall send forth his mighty winds, yea, his shafts in the whirlwind, yea, when all his hail and his mighty storm shall beat upon you, it shall have no power over you to drag you down to the gulf of misery and endless wo, because of the rock upon which ye are built, which is a sure foundation, a foundation whereon if men build they cannot fail. (Helaman 5:12)

Power to Regroup:

To receive more truth

> And therefore, he that will harden his heart, the same receiveth the lesser portion of the word; and he that will not harden his heart, to him is given the greater portion of the word, until it is given unto him to know the mysteries of God until he know them in full. (Alma 12:10)

To become the children of God

> But verily, verily, I say unto you, that as many as receive me, to them will I give power to become the sons [and daughters] of God, even to them that believe on my name. Amen. (D&C 11:30)

Elder Bruce R. McConkie said, "We have the power—and it is our privilege—so to live, that becoming pure in heart, we shall see the face of God while we yet dwell as mortals in a world of sin and sorrow" *(Conference Report,* October 1977, p. 34).

Power to Respond:

To teach with the Spirit

> But this is not all; they had given themselves to much prayer, and fasting; there-

fore they had the spirit of prophecy, and the spirit of revelation, and when they taught, they taught with power and authority of God. (Alma 17:3)

To teach with power

"And now, as the preaching of the word had a great tendency to lead the people to do that which was just—yea, it had had more powerful effect upon the minds of the people than the sword, or anything else, which had happened unto them—therefore Alma thought it was expedient that they should try the virtue of the word of God." (Alma 31:5)

As we participate in this power, we realize its effect on us and those we serve. Notice the effect it had on Wilford Woodruff and those he taught:

On Sunday, the 8th, I preached at Frome's Hill in the morning, at Standley Hill in the afternoon, and at John Benbow's, Hill Farm, in the evening. The parish church that stood in the neighborhood of Brother Benbow's, presided over by the rector of the parish, was attended during the day by only fifteen persons, while I had a large congregation, estimated to number a thousand, attend my meetings through the day and evening.

When I arose to speak at Brother Benbow's house, a man entered the door and informed me that he was a constable, and had been sent by the rector of the parish with a warrant to arrest me. I asked him, "For what crime?" He said, "For preaching to the people." I told him that I, as well as the rector, had a license for preaching the gospel to the people, and that if he would take a chair I would wait upon him after meeting. He took my chair and sat beside me. For an hour and a quarter I preached the first principles of the everlasting gospel. The power of God rested upon me, the spirit filled the house, and the people were convinced. At the close of the meeting I opened the door for baptism, and seven offered themselves. Among the number were four preachers and the constable. The latter arose and said, "Mr. Woodruff, I would like to be baptized." I told him I would like to baptize him. I went down into the pool and baptized the seven. We then came together. I confirmed thirteen, administered the Sacrament, and we all rejoiced together.

The constable went to the rector and told him that if he wanted Mr. Woodruff taken for preaching the gospel, he must go himself and serve the writ; for he had heard him preach the only true gospel sermon he had ever listened to in his life. The rector did not know what to make of it, so he sent two clerks of the Church of England as spies, to attend our meeting, and find out what we did preach. They both were pricked in their hearts, received the word of the Lord gladly, and were baptized and confirmed members of the Church of Jesus Christ of Latter-day Saints. The rector became alarmed, and did not venture to send anybody else. (*Wilford Woodruff: History of His Life And Labors*, pp. 117-18)

This real knowledge of the past, present, and future blesses us with a confidence that is manifest in many areas of our lives (see D&C 93:24). We are able to resist temptation, regroup with the Spirit, and respond to those who need our help.

In 2 Timothy 3:16, we learn that all scripture is given by inspiration and is profitable for man; for doctrine, reproof, correction, and instruction. Knowing the doctrine, we understand truth. We are reproved when we are out of harmony with the truth, and then we are corrected as needed and instructed in paths of righteousness.

Our Eternal Father wants us to learn and know His doctrine. He "and His Beloved Son are willing, even anxious for us to learn from them. . . . Gaining spiritual knowledge is not a mechanical process. It is a sacred privilege based upon spiritual law" (Richard G. Scott, *Ensign,* November 1993, p. 88).

We need to be in constant pursuit of truth in order to possess its power. The Lord wants us to obtain His truths so that we may stand up to temptation. We, like the young woman named Elizabeth discussed earlier, should not wait to prepare. Elizabeth had already learned her response to temptation, and the Spirit drew it out in her time of need. The scriptures teach us to treasure up the truths that will give us spiritual power: "Neither take ye thought beforehand what ye shall say; but treasure up in your minds continually the words of life, and it shall be given you in the very hour that portion that shall be meted unto every man" (D&C 84:85).

In conclusion, I would like to share a thought about the importance of knowing the truth.

> He who knows not that he knows not—is a fool;
>   Shun him.
> He who knows that he knows not—is seeking;
>   Teach him.
> He who knows not that he knows—is asleep;
>   Awake him.
> He who knows that he knows—is a wise man;
>   Follow him.
>
> Arabian Proverb

May we treasure the truth by our personal preparation to receive truth, by our energetic pursuit of truth, and by our use of the power of truth.

Chapter Three

You Feel and Follow
the Promptings of the Spirit

You have probably noticed those members of the Church who cry all through fast and testimony meeting. They are so touched, the rivers of tears just keep on flowing. Some of my own family members like to "water the podium." I've always felt bad that I have not had this same experience. For some reason, when I got my opportunity to stand, I would get this geeky grin on my face as I expressed joy in the gospel. Don't get me wrong, I have cried before. But I am what I call a closet crier. I go where no one else can see me. As I began learning about the workings of the Spirit, I realized that I *was* having a similar experience–my reaction was just different.

As I have observed various Church leaders, I have come to understand that *tears are not the gauge for spiritual experiences.* Sometimes they are just one individual's reaction to the Spirit. People having the same spiritual experience could respond in different ways. Some seem to never cry, while others never speak without crying. One person might smile, another might cry, and yet others might simply bow their head in contemplation.

I would like to explore five concepts that will help us understand how to feel and follow the promptings of the Spirit: *misconceptions, impersonations, manifestations, applications,* and *invitations.*

MISCONCEPTIONS

Once upon a time I heard a wonderful faith-promoting rumor. However, even though the individual sharing it was quite choked up, I did not believe it. It was the first time I heard it, but it was not the last. I have since heard about it occurring in different states with different individuals involved. It is probably a rumor you have heard of, but I would like to summarize one of the common versions.

It always begins with someone returning home from a temple. The driver sees a hitchhiker on a freeway, and for some strange reason, he or she feels impressed to pick him up. The person rides in the back seat for a while and then asks, "Do you have your food storage?" The driver is told to hurry and get it, then the person disappears. Sometimes the story includes the appearance of the police, who are puzzled with reports of frequent visits.

These stories seem to float all around the Church. They are not circulated through general conference, but in conversations with other Church members when someone is trying to make an impact. Now, can you imagine a council in heaven where an angel is given the assignment of hitchhiking on Interstate 80? This particular story has been around at least since the fifties and in recent years local newspapers have referred back to this legend. But these spiritual fables do not appear to be consistent with validated spiritual practices. President Harold B. Lee said:

> When there is to be anything different from that which the Lord has told us already, he will give it to his prophet, not to some Tom, Dick, or Harry, [who] is thumbing his way across the country as we have had people tell the story; and not through someone, as another story relates, who swooned and came up and gave a revelation. (*Living Prophets for a Living Church*, p. 189-91)

In general conference, President Harold B. Lee also said, "It never ceases to amaze me how gullible some of our Church members are in broadcasting these sensational stories, or dreams, or visions. . . ." *(Conference Report,* October 1972, p. 126; or *Ensign,* January 1973, p. 105)

In the Book of Mormon, 2 Nephi chapter 28 we are taught about some common spiritual misconceptions. Nephi said, concerning the people in the last days, that–

They will say there are no such things as miracles (see verse 6).

They will believe that they can do whatever they want, and everything will be okay (see verse 7).

They will say that God will allow a little sin (see verse 8).

They will teach that God's punishment is insignificant, and He will make exceptions for them (see verse 8).

They will think they can hide their sins from Lord (see verse 9).

Their spirituality will be based on worldly success and security (see verse 21).

They will believe that their conduct is okay because it is only natural human behavior (see verse 22).

When we hear these misconceptions, we should be so familiar with the workings of the Spirit, that we pay them no heed. Elder Marion G. Romney specified instructions to assist in detecting counterfeits:

> "Anything purporting to pertain to the Gospel of Jesus Christ may be put to the following four simple tests":
>
> 1. *Is it of God or man?* . . . If it originated in the wisdom of men, it is not of God. . . .
> 2. *Does the teaching bear the proper label?* . . . If any teaching purporting to be from Christ comes under any label other than that of Jesus Christ, we can know it is not of God. . . .
> 3. *Does it conform to the other teaching of the gospel of Jesus Christ?*
> 4. *Does it come through the proper Church channels?* (*Conference Report,* October 1960, pp. 76-77)

In the Book of Mormon, Moroni warned us to beware not to judge evil to be from God, or good to be of the devil (see Moroni 7:14). He then taught us the way to judge between good and evil. He said:

> For behold, the Spirit of Christ is given to every man, that he may know good from evil; wherefore, I show unto you the way to judge; for everything which inviteth to do good, and to persuade to believe in Christ, is sent forth by the power and gift of Christ; wherefore ye may know with a perfect knowledge it is of God.
>
> But whatsoever thing persuadeth men to do evil, and believe not in Christ, and deny him, and serve not God, then ye may know with a perfect knowledge it is of the devil; for after this manner doth the devil work, for he persuadeth no man to do good, no, not one; neither do his angels; neither do they who subject themselves unto him. (Moroni 7:16-17)

IMPERSONATIONS

I've always been intrigued with impersonators. The only impersonations I can do are poor versions of Kermit the Frog and Darth Vader. I'm amazed with those who sound identical to the famous person they are imitating. But they are still not the real thing. President Boyd K. Packer said, "There are counterfeit spirits as there are counterfeit angels. . . . The spiritual part of us and the emotional part of us are so closely linked that it is possible to mistake an emotional impulse for something spiritual" (*Ensign*, January 1983, pp. 55-56). Sometimes what we are feeling is simply an impersonation, even if the feeling brings us to tears. Sometimes what others may be feeling is an impersonation, even if they have tears. We need to look for the tried and tested feelings of the Spirit, taught to us in the scriptures and in the words of the living prophets. Even though promptings from the Spirit come in many ways, President Spencer W. Kimball taught that the most common methods are less spectacular. He said, "In our day, as in times past, many people . . . expect if there be revelation it will come with awe-inspiring, earth-shaking display. . . ." *(Conference Report*, April 1997, p. 115). He continues:

> The burning bushes, . . . the Cumorahs, and the Kirtlands were realities; but they were the exceptions. The great volume of revelation came to Moses and to Joseph and comes to today's prophet in the less spectacular way—that of deep impressions, without spectacle or glamour or dramatic events. Always expecting the spectacular, many will miss entirely the constant flow of revealed communication. (*Conference Report*, Munich Germany Area Conference, 1973, pp. 76-77)

When people look for the sensational and spectacular, they are setting themselves up to be misled. Often people who use these extraordinary stories are trying to influence someone for good, but the tactic itself is not of God. Some of our youth lose hope in their own spiritual abilities because they have not had those same sensational incidents that others claim. Unfortunately, even though the teacher or friend with good intentions is trying to show the power of the Spirit by sharing an amazing story, they are actually removing hope. Too many people become bored with the idea of gaining spiritual strength by fasting, prayer, and reading the scriptures—they begin to expect the extraordinary. Joseph Fielding McConkie said:

> Spirituality is something to be worked at, not something to be played with. Satan can and does use such expressions as "I feel impressed to say," "It was made known to me," "After much prayer," and "It is the will of the Lord that. . . ." Satan, who can

speak all languages, also speaks very fluent Mormonese.

Truth can stand on its own. . . . It does not need an office or a position to lean on. . . . It is not enhanced by show of force, nor is it made more recognizable by emotional displays. Everything that comes from God carries with it its own evidence of its divine origin and needs no artificial coloring to make it more palatable. (*The Spirit of Revelation* [Salt Lake City: Deseret Book, 1984], p. 127)

We cannot afford to be unfamiliar with the Spirit or misled. In general conference, Marion G. Romney taught several points concerning the promptings of the Spirit. For instance:

PROMPTINGS:
- Do not violate any gospel principles (including the free agency of another).
- Are in harmony with teachings of the scriptures and prophets.
- Are in harmony with the order of the Church.
- Bring peace to the soul.
- Do not raise doubts and questions.
- Result in lasting happiness when we follow them.
- May be contrary to our own desires when we are asking for the wrong things. (See *Conference Report*, October 1960, pp. 76-77.)

President Harold B. Lee cautioned the members of the Church by saying, "If our people want to be safely guided during these troublous times of deceit and false rumors, they must follow their leaders and seek for the guidance of the Spirit of the Lord in order to avoid falling prey to clever manipulators. . . ." (*Conference Report*, October 1972, p. 126; or *Ensign*, January 1973, p. 105).

MANIFESTATIONS

The Spirit *comforts* us, *teaches* us, *warns* us, *testifies to* us, and *improves* us.

The Spirit comforts us.

On November 3, 1973, my brother-in-law, Leonard Dobson, was flying home from his full-time mission on a National Airlines DC10. Leonard had converted to the Church when he was twenty-six-years-old and was already a civil engineer. But now it was time to come home.

Because of his interest in science, Leonard enjoyed his window seat nearest the engine, not surprising for someone who graduated in engineering. During a layover in Houston, Leonard got up to talk with the pilot and flight engineer, and when he returned to his seat, he found that someone else had taken it. The individual apologized for taking Leonard's seat, but Leonard simply volunteered to move a few rows up to a vacant seat next to another window.

As the flight continued, a large explosion came suddenly and unexpectedly from one of the jet-engines. The passengers began screaming with fear. The window next to Leonard's original seat was shattered by a piece of metal during the explosion. Leonard's first thought was that he was going to die in a plane crash, so he began to pray. As he prayed, he was comforted. Instead of fear, he began to feel confidence in the Lord. Using his fingertips, he pried open the oxygen mask compartment, which had failed to open. Feeling particularly calm, he had a desire to help others. Some of the people did not have oxygen masks, and others had fainted, allowing their masks to fall from their faces. Leonard started to get up to help until he was directed by the flight attendant to sit down and buckle up.

While others were screaming, fainting, and stunned with shock, Leonard was comforted by the Spirit, and he began taking priceless pictures of the engine as it fell apart.

Finally the passengers on the plane were instructed to get in the crash-landing position. As Leonard sat there, the Spirit brought promises from his patriarchal blessing to his mind, that he would be a father and have a family, and that he would be able to teach his own family the gospel. Calmly, Leonard sat with his head between his knees until the plane finally touched down in Albuquerque, New Mexico. Only when the other passengers quickly slid down the emergency chutes did they finally feel secure.

There is a very unfortunate part to this story. The man who sat in Leonard's first seat was sucked through the broken window by the force of decompression. (Part of Leonard's story was in the *New Era*, January 1974, pp. 18-19.)

The Spirit can comfort us. We can be in a situation like Leonard and still be calm in the middle of terror. Such is the power of the Spirit. James E. Faust said, "I believe the Spirit of the Holy Ghost is the greatest guarantor of inward peace in our unstable world. It can be more mind-expanding and can make us have a better sense of well-being than any chemical or other earthly substance. It will calm nerves; it will breathe peace to our souls" *(Conference Report,* April 1989, p. 41).

The Spirit teaches us.

I had an experience while I was helping to build my house. I was doing the tile work—600 square feet. I had never laid tile before, but I was trying to save some money. Late one Saturday night, my son Tyson and I were almost done with the job. We had to be finished before Monday, and the next day was the Sabbath. It was about 11:30 p.m. and we had been working all day. Tyson was doing the cutting and I was laying the tile. We arrived at the spot that was the most difficult—the pantry. The pantry had been built with angles, and we could not figure out how to cut the tile so it would fit around the angled doorway. Because he was tired, Tyson asked if we could quit and go home. I reminded him we had to have the job done by Monday, and neither of us wanted to work on the Sabbath. He had already attempted to cut tile to fit, but each time the tile had either broken or did not look good enough. I told him to try it one more time.

While he was downstairs trying to do the impossible, I knelt down in the pantry and asked my Father in Heaven for some help. In the prayer, I mentioned that we did not have time to go for help, we did not want to work on Sunday, and we did not know what to do. Does Heavenly Father care about tile? He must, because I had no sooner said, "Amen," and a great idea popped into my mind. As Tyson came back upstairs, I told him, "I know what to do." It was so simple.

We finished the job and it looked great. In fact, a few days later while I was out of town, some tile workers stopped by my house and told my wife that the pantry area looked great. Now every time I look in the pantry, I have a reminder of how much Heavenly Father cares about me.

In section 8 of the Doctrine and Covenants, Oliver Cowdery received a revelation from the Lord through the prophet Joseph. He was told:

> Oliver Cowdery, verily, verily, I say unto you, that assuredly as the Lord liveth, who is your God and your Redeemer, even so *surely shall you receive a knowledge of whatsoever things you shall ask in faith, with an honest heart, believing that you shall receive* a knowledge concerning the engravings of old records, which are ancient, which contain those parts of my scripture of which has been spoken *by the manifestation of my Spirit.*
>
> *Yea, behold, I will tell you in your mind and in your heart, by the Holy Ghost, which shall come upon you and which shall dwell in your heart.* (D&C 8:1-2; emphasis added)

The Spirit teaches us what we need to know, and sometimes what we want to know. It is up to us to be listening. In the

October 1973 general conference, H. Burke Peterson said, "Answers from the Lord come quietly—ever so quietly. In fact, few hear his answers audibly with their ears. We must be listening so carefully or we will never recognize them. Most answers from the Lord are felt in our heart as a warm comfortable expression, or . . . as thoughts to our mind. They come to those who are prepared and who are patient" *(Conference Report,* October 1973, p. 13).

The Spirit warns us.

Speaking about the Spirit, Neal A. Maxwell said, "Sometimes what comes is almost a warning shout, especially when hearers are unstirred by the still, small voice" *(Conference Report,* October 1986, p. 72). The Spirit warns us of dangers, and helps us to be advised and protected. My dad fell asleep once while driving. He had drifted into the oncoming lanes when he heard a loud voice yell, "Wake up!"

Listen to how beautifully President David O. McKay encouraged us to accept this guidance. He said, "God help us so to live that we may be found worthy to hear from him the whisperings of his Spirit, the whisperings of his voice, as he guides us and warns us and tells us what to do in order to come back into his presence" *(Conference Report,* October 1968, p.145).

The Spirit testifies to us.

In her own words, a young girl named Mary Field talked about an important time in Church history that the Spirit testified to her. She said:

> After Joseph's death there was some confusion as to who should be our leader. Sidney Rigdon claimed to have had a vision that he should be our leader, but I, with my mother, was present at the meeting in the bowery when the mantel of Joseph fell upon Brigham Young while he was talking to the people. Mother had the baby on her knee.

While the baby was playing with a tin cup he dropped it, attracting our attention to the floor. Mother stooped over to pick it up. We were startled by hearing the voice of Joseph. Looking up quickly we saw the form of the Prophet Joseph standing before us. . . . There was no doubt in the hearts of the Saints from that moment on who was to be their inspired leader. . . . ("The Last Leaf: Life of Mary Field Garner," written by Annie Gardner Barton, p. 4. *Note:* This story is mentioned in *Guide to Mormon Diaries and Autobiographies,* Davis Bitton, Provo, Utah, BYU Press, 1977. Original transcript is in the Harold B. Lee Library, Brigham Young University. The spelling and grammar are as they appear in the original.)

Mary Field Garner was my grandmother's grandmother. She felt and experienced a witness that influenced my life.

The Spirit testifies of truth. Bishop Keith B. McMullin said, "A millennium of experience through sight, sound, touch, taste, smell and all the powers of the universe combined cannot approach the sublime and complete experience of one brief moment under the influence of the Holy Ghost" *(Ensign,* May 1996, p. 9).

The Spirit improves us.

Heavenly Father wants a willing heart, and He will take care of the rest. In general conference in April 1989, James E. Faust said,

This comforter can be with us as we seek to improve . . . and [it] also helps keep us from making mistakes. It can enhance our natural senses so that we can see more clearly, hear more keenly, and remember what we should remember. It is a way of maximizing our happiness. (*Conference Report,* April 1989, p. 41)

Parley P. Pratt said,

> The gift of the Holy Ghost . . . quickens all the
> intellectual faculties, increases, enlarges, expands,
> and purifies all the natural passions and affections,
> and adapts them, by the gift of wisdom, to their
> lawful use. It inspires, develops, cultivates, and
> matures all the fine-toned sympathies, joys, tastes,
> kindred feelings, and affections of our nature. It
> inspires virtue, kindness, goodness, tenderness,
> gentleness, and charity. It develops beauty of
> person, form, and features. It tends to health, vigor,
> animation, and social feeling. It invigorates all the
> faculties of the physical and intellectual man. It
> strengthens and gives tone to the nerves. In short, it
> is, as it were, marrow to the bone, joy to the heart,
> light to the eyes, music to the ears, and life to the
> whole being. *(Key to the Science of Theology* [Salt
> Lake City: Deseret Book, 1978], p. 61)

No wonder Marion G. Romney said, "The key to happiness is to get the Spirit and keep it" *(Conference Report,* October 61, p. 61).

APPLICATIONS

When you have the Spirit, you feel happy, calm, and clear-minded. You feel that nobody can offend you. You would not mind if everyone could see your actions. You feel like praying (see 2 Nephi 32:8). A desire to keep all the commandments comes upon you. You feel confidently in control and very glad to be alive.

When you don't have the Spirit, you feel frustrated, confused, and depressed. You become selfish and do not want to share your time. You become easily offended and try to hide your secret actions. The desire to pray leaves you, and you feel restricted by all those "silly" commandments. You begin to wonder if life is really worth it.

If we find ourselves in a situation where we do not have the Spirit, we must make a change. George Q. Cannon said, "Whenever darkness fills our minds, we may know that we are not possessed of the Spirit of God, and we must get rid of it. When we are filled with the Spirit of God, we are filled with joy, with peace, and with happiness no matter what our circumstances may be; for it is a spirit of cheerfulness and happiness. . . ." *(Gospel Truth,* 1:20).

INVITATIONS

In the Book of Mormon, Alma extends an essential invitation concerning the Spirit. He said:

> And now, my brethren, I wish from the inmost part of my heart, yea, with great anxiety even unto pain, that ye would hearken unto my words, and cast off your sins, and not procrastinate the day of your repentance;
>
> But that ye would humble yourselves before the Lord, and call on his holy name, and watch and pray continually, that ye may not be tempted above that which ye can bear, *and thus be led by the Holy Spirit, becoming humble, meek, submissive, patient, full of love and all long-suffering;*
>
> *Having faith on the Lord; having a hope that ye shall receive eternal life; having the love of God always in your hearts,* that ye may be lifted up at the last day and enter into his rest. (Alma 13:27-29; emphasis added)

We need to obtain and maintain the guidance of the Holy Spirit. Elder M. Russell Ballard talked about this need when he said, "We must have personal, spiritual experiences to anchor us. These come through seeking them in the same intense, single-minded way that a hungry person seeks food" *(Ensign,* May

1996, p. 80). Marion G. Romney taught four principles for obtaining this special guidance,

> First, Pray diligently . . . in great faith and confidence.
> Second, Study and learn the gospel.
> Third, Live righteously, repent . . . [and] conform to . . . the gospel.
> Fourth, Give service in the Church. (*Ensign,* January 1980, p. 5)

Don't give up while you are learning to find answers. The Lord is in charge, not us. Elder Boyd K. Packer said, "It may be that you are not doing anything wrong. It may be that you have not done the right things long enough. Remember, you cannot force spiritual things" ("Prayers and Answers," *Ensign,* November 1979, p. 21). If we try to force a relationship with the Spirit, we can set ourselves up for deception. We must keep living the fundamentals of the gospel and "Wait on the Lord" (see Psalm 37:34). Elder Packer said:

> Carry a prayer in your heart always.
> Let sleep come every night with your mind centered in prayer.
> Keep the Word of Wisdom.
> Read the scriptures.
> Listen to your parents and to the leaders of the Church.
> Stay away from places and things that common sense tells you will interfere with inspiration.
> Develop your spiritual capacities.
> Learn to tune out the static and the interference.
> Avoid the substitutes and the counterfeits!
> *Learn to be inspired and directed by the Holy Ghost.*
> (*Conference Report,* October 1979, p. 30; emphasis added)

Chapter Four

You Enjoy This Expedition Called Life

Embarrassing things happen. They happen to all of us, and we've all felt the impact they have on our self-esteem. Once, when I was about fourteen years old, I was watching my sister's children in her back yard while she was in the house. The kids where playing on the swing set as I was doing pull-ups in between the bolts holding up the set of swings. It was summer time so I was dressed in a tank-top and cut-offs (common attire for the seventies). I would begin by grabbing the bar with my hands and then hang with my arms outstretched. I would pull myself up between the swings, then rest my waist on the bar. Then to get back down, I would spin around the bar, quickly dropping to the starting position. It was like a gymnastic maneuver, and I did it over and over again. I got to where I could spin really fast; it was quite the sensation.

Then it happened. While I was spinning as fast as I could, the belt loop on my cutoffs caught a bolt sticking out of the top of the swing set crossbar. Because of the speed of my spin, when the belt loop got caught, it ripped the crotch right out of my cut-offs. I slid through the cut-offs, and was left hanging with the cut-offs twisted around my arms. I began to yell for help. My little niece and nephew were not big enough to give me any assistance, so I continued to yell for my sister. You'd think she would have been a little concerned for my safety and well being, but as she got closer to me and saw me hanging in my boxers, she began laughing hysterically.

That was not the first time something embarrassing has happened to me. Nor would it be the last. While sitting in my high school math class, I was talking with a young lady because the teacher had left the room. I'm sure we were discussing integers and whole numbers. (Yeah, right!) As we were talking, I was sitting with my elbows on my knees and my fists on my cheeks. (I call this the Aaronic Priesthood position; if you look around in church on Sunday, you will notice several of the young men sitting this way.) Suddenly, as I looked down to the tile floor, I accidentally drooled. Right in front of this girl.

I kept my eyes looking down, not making any quick movements. And slowly looked up to see if she noticed. By the look on her face I could tell that she had. I was so embarrassed, but I was not going to let her think that I was. So I rubbed the slobber with the bottom of my foot and pretended that I did it on purpose. And just to make sure she thought I did it on purpose, I spat on the floor again and rubbed it with my foot again.

Now, at the time, I thought it was a great idea. She would not think that I accidentally slobbered on the floor; instead, she would think I purposely spat on the school floor.

Now experiences like this can really take a toll on your self-esteem. And further, if this young lady were to go about the school telling everyone that I spit on floors, she might create a reputation for me that would also affect my self-esteem. Some people might say to themselves, "I've never seen him do that before," or others might believe her. But I don't spit on floors, I don't usually slobber, and I'd be the only one who really knows the truth. Self-esteem, therefore, is your own reputation with yourself. It's what you know about you. It is a feeling of self-endorsement. A feeling that you approve of who you really are. It's this self-endorsement that helps us handle embarrassing situations. But self-esteem is much more than this. This is just the beginning. For me, self-esteem is made up of several elements: *Be Personal, Be Progressive, Be Positive, Be Prepared, Be Powerful,* and *Be Your Potential.* I put it this way: *Personally progressing* with a *positive* attitude while *preparing* to protect our *powerful potential.*

BE PERSONAL

Ask yourself this question, "Do I like myself?" If the answer is yes, then you have achieved the first step in self-esteem—a feeling of self-worth. But if you answered no, you must begin to realize the person that you are. If we liken the scriptures unto ourselves as we are taught to do, then we find insight in Isaiah 42:4, which reads, "Since thou wast precious in my sight, thou hast been honorable, and I have loved thee. . . ." We need to remember how much our Heavenly Father loves us. He gave His son for us (see John 3:16).

I remember hearing part of the lyrics of a song titled "Leave It Like It Is" by a singer named Dave Wilcox. In the third verse he sings, "Most folks suffer in sorrow, thinking they're just no good. They don't match the magazine model as close as they think they should. They live just like a paint by numbers; the teacher would be impressed. A lifetime of 'follow the line,' so it's just like all the rest."

No, we are not the same, and we don't have the same abilities, attributes, and talents, but we are loved and created by God. He made us. We were not meant to be a paint by numbers; rather, each one of us was meant to be a masterpiece. The evidence of this masterpiece is in our fingerprints. We are all individuals and individually loved by our Father in Heaven. We need to go through this expedition of life, happy to be ourselves.

> Don't be what you ain't
> jes' be what you is.
> 'Cuz if you is not what you am
> den you am not what you is.
>
> If you is jes' a little tadpole
> don't try to be a frog.

If you is jes' the tail
don't try to wag de dog.

You can always pass the plate
if you can't exhort and preach.
If you is jes' a pebble
don't try to be the beach.

Don't be what you ain't
jes' be what you is.
'Cuz de man dat plays it square
am goin' to get what's his;
It ain't what you all has been
it's what you all now is!
So don't be what you ain't
jes be what you is!!

–Author Unknown

BE PROGRESSIVE

Even though we should be happy to be ourselves, we have to take a look at reality and progress from that point. Reality creates an accurate foundation for motivation. To look yourself in the mirror and say, "I'm good enough, I'm smart enough, and dog-gone-it, people like me," may be a start, but it's not enough. We have to improve. If we put our foot in our mouth, should we just say, "Well that's just who I am"? Or should we try not to make the same mistake in the future? To identify a personal weakness is not to *lack* self-esteem, but to *apply* self-esteem.

In 2 Corinthians 12:10, the apostle Paul says, "Therefore I take pleasure in infirmities, in reproaches, in distresses for Christ's sake: for when I am weak, then am I strong." This life is all about being open to improvement. Be happy to be your real self, then progress from there. Sister Camilla Kimball, President Kimball's wife said:

> The Lord does not judge us by what we have but by
> what we do with what we have. The rich may be
> haughty, the poor envious, the powerful cruel,
> the weak sniveling. And those between the
> extremes may well be complacent and lukewarm. . . .
> To be rich is good, if you can be humble.
> To be learned is good, if you can be wise.
> To be healthy is good, if you can be useful.
> To be beautiful is good, if you can be gracious.
> There is, however, nothing inherently bad in being
> poor, unlettered, sickly, or plain.
> To be poor is good, if you can still be generous of spirit.
> To be unschooled is good, if it motivates you to be curious.
> To be sickly is good, if it helps you to have compassion.
> To be plain is good, if it saves you from vanity.
> *(Ye Are Free To Choose,* pamphlet)

As we notice our real weakness, and then work toward improvement, we are exercising our self-esteem. Not that we are not
happy to be ourselves, but we are working at being our best self.

BE POSITIVE

One of the big problems people have with self-esteem is
comparing themselves with others. We usually see others at their
best and compare our worst with their best. For example, if I were
introducing my best friend, Ed Eyestone, as a speaker, I would
share many of his greatest accomplishments. I would want the
audience to know who they would be listening to. I would say:

> Ed Eyestone was born in Ogden, Utah, and
> attended Bonneville High School.
> He was student body vice-president and partici-
> pated in many school activities.
> He was undefeated in high-school cross-country
> for two years.

He won state by over a minute, setting a state record.

As a freshman in college, he was the number one man on BYU's cross-country team.

He took third place in the world junior cross-country championships in France.

Throughout college he was a ten-time All-American.

He was a four-time NCAA champion: cross-country, 5,000 meters, and twice in the 10,000 meters.

He holds the American collegiate record in the 10,000 meters.

He has been in two Olympics, 1988 and 1992.

He has been the American Runner of the Year five times.

Many of us have the tendency to compare others' greatest accomplishments with our failures. Imagine now that Ed has just spoken, and now we will hear from Michael W. Allred. The person introducing me could say,

Michael Weir Allred was born in Ogden, Utah, and attended Bonneville High School.

He played football, as a defensive lineman, and at 5'10" and 167 pounds, he feels very blessed to be alive today.

It isn't surprising that he was not All-State.

He was a varsity wrestler, but finished his senior year with a record of 3 wins, 13 losses, and one knock-out. He was knocked out and taken to the hospital after leading the match 12-3.

He was cut from the high school tennis team and was never considered senior best at anything.

Like his closest friends, Mike was also elected to school government but was dismissed for academic reasons.

His best friend, Ed Eyestone, was a college All-American and participated in two Olympics, while Mike is about 20 pounds overweight and has a receding hairline.

With a list of failures like that, how could anyone have any self-esteem? The point is, that with real self-esteem, it isn't how many times you fall, but how often you get back up and try again. We need to stay positive and not compare ourselves. Remember, a rosebush is judged by its flowers, not by its thorns.

As individuals, we all have different blessings and talents. However, because we live in a world that places a high value on people in the spotlight, like Michael Jordan and Julia Roberts, many youth feel that the only talents worth having are in sports or the arts. But what about the talent of being a good friend? Or the talent of being a great spouse? Do we really value these gifts? Imagine sitting in a high school classroom on the beginning day of school, and the teacher asks everyone to share their name and give one of their talents. It would sound something like this:

> "Hey, my name is Rick, and I'm the quarterback on the football team."
>
> "Hi, my name is Steve, and I'm the Math Sterling Scholar."
>
> "Hi, you guys. My name is Jennifer, but you all know that. I'm the head cheerleader. Hope to see you out at the game Friday night. Go team! Whoah!"
>
> "Yo! My name is Frank, and that's my cherry '67 Super Sport in the parking lot."
>
> "I'm Vince, and I love to paint."
>
> "I'm Lisa, and I don't have any talents."

I can't tell you how many times I have heard that last line. So many kids think because they don't sing, dance, or play sports, they have no talents. I would like to hear a similar discussion at a school that sounds like this:

> "Hey, my name is Rick, and I get along well with my mom."
>
> "Hi, my name is Steve, and I love to do service projects and homework."
>
> "Hi, everyone! I'm Jennifer, and I like to make people happy."
>
> "Yo, my name is Frank, and I like talking with my family."
>
> "I'm Vince, and I like to hang out with my little brother. He's awesome."
>
> "I'm Lisa, and I'm a great friend."

Notice the difference, and ask yourself which talents will make the world a better place? There is nothing wrong with being a cheerleader, quarterback, or scholar. But there is something wrong when a person who gets along well with his mom says he doesn't have any talents. Stay positive!

BE PREPARED

While I was living in Idaho, a close friend invited me to go bow hunting with him. I did not have a bow and I had never gone before. In fact, I had never seriously shot a compound bow. My friend Rob assured me that he would get a bow for me and teach me how to use it. I said I would go, so he instructed me how to get human smells out of my camouflage clothes. The week quickly passed, and one morning Rob came by to pick me up. He pulled a bow from the back of a little pickup truck and said, "Let's go." I informed him that I still had not shot a bow yet. He then took me to the neighbor's yard, where they had a target set up, and he taught me how to aim. My first shot missed not only the target, but the compressed boxes the target was fastened to. My second shot also missed everything. At last, my third shot hit the boxes. It still missed the target, but at least we did not have to go looking for this one. He said, "Okay, you're ready." He knew I really wasn't.

We arrived late that night and set up camp. I was really looking forward to this experience. I did not sleep well in anticipation of getting an elk or maybe even a deer. I didn't have a lot of money, and I knew a large animal would give me a lot of meat. My friend and I woke up early before the sun, camouflaged our faces, and left camp. I went up one mountain, and he went up another. Because of my lack of experience, I walked too fast and made a lot of noise. When the day was over, Rob advised me not to make so much noise. Then he taught me how to walk and move more quietly.

I took the next day off for the Sabbath, but on Monday morning I was ready to go again. This time I crept up the mountain. I moved so slowly I could hear all the birds singing and the breeze blowing. It was very serene. As I arrived at the top of a draw, I felt so calm that I wanted to pray. I removed my hat and thanked my Father in Heaven for a beautiful world. I thanked Him for my family and for the opportunities I have in life. Of course, before I finished I also pleaded for the chance to get an elk. I stood up, put on my hat, and began sneaking across the mountain.

I had only gone about twenty steps when my prayer was answered. At first, I thought I saw the back end of a horse on the other side of a tree, but then I realized it was a cow elk. I began saying a prayer of thanks in my heart, and my legs turned to rubber. I was about two hundred yards from the elk so I slowly moved from tree to tree, hoping she wouldn't notice me. My legs were so shaky that I was sure I would step on a twig, but I was getting closer and closer. I was about eighty yards from her when I finally stepped on a twig. Snap! I peeked around the tree I was next to and saw that she was looking around for me although she couldn't see me. She started quietly walking up the mountain in the other direction, and again I prayed in my heart, asking Heavenly Father for another chance. I explained, "I'm sorry that my abilities are not equal to your blessing, but please give me another chance."

The elk turned around and started coming back toward me. My heart was shouting prayers of thanks. I couldn't believe it. I asked to get an elk, and there she was. After making one mistake, I asked for another chance, and here she came again. Not only did she come to within forty yards of me, but when she stopped, she turned broadside. I knelt down and drew my bow. I could see her looking around for me, and could even see her wet, shiny nose. She was a large beautiful animal and would easily fill my food storage needs. It was so perfect; it was as if she was saying, "Come on, give it your best shot."

Well that's just what I did. I let that arrow go. My arrow went flying, but not only did I miss the vital area on this huge elk, I missed the whole elk by about three yards. I really missed. But boy, did I scare her! She let out a cry and took off running. Again, I began to pray, "Why, Heavenly Father? Why?" And at that point, it was as if a voice spoke in my mind, answering, "You took no thought save to ask me."

I learned a great lesson in life. We are blessed from our Father above, but we still have to do our part. We must prepare ourselves for those opportunities that we wish to succeed in. Remember what it says in James 2:26, "Faith without works is dead."

BE POWERFUL

Someone once told me that self-esteem is like an immune system. It serves to protect us from the challenges of the world. Not that it helps us avoid trials, but it helps us handle them. When we have this confidence, we can make things happen, instead of just watching what happens to us. Sterling W. Sill said, "There is no power in the universe that can come between us and the celestial kingdom, except our own power" (*Conference Report*, October 1975, p. 42). That must be why section ten of Doctrine and Covenants teaches us to "pray always that [we] might come off conqueror" (see D&C 10:5). Our power and self-esteem increases when we understand ourselves and our relationship to Christ.

> . . . In all these things we are more than conquerors through him that loved us. For I am persuaded, that neither death, nor life, nor angels, nor principalities, nor powers, nor things present, nor things to come, Nor height, nor depth, nor any other creature, shall be able to separate us from the love of God, which is in Christ Jesus our Lord. (Romans 8:37-39)

With self-esteem we become strong in our success and failures. Ed Eystone began running because he was cut from a junior high baseball team. Babe Ruth is known for how many home runs he hit, not how many times he struck out. Abraham Lincoln is known for being a great president, not for all the political defeats on his way there. When opposition is strong, we need to be powerful throughout the wins and the losses. Remember, we progress on a cycle that spirals upward toward our potential.

BE YOUR POTENTIAL

Our potential is a frontier to be discovered and explored. The joy of life is in the expedition. Isn't it fun to find out just how good we can get at something? Not just succeeding in the things of this earth, but learning about our divine nature as literal children of our Heavenly Father. That means we can become like him. What great potential we have! I saw a poster once that said, "What lies behind us and what lies before us are tiny matters compared to what lies within us." We are to become like our Father. That is what lies within us.

In Romans 8:16-17 we read, "The Spirit itself beareth witness with our spirit, that we are the children of God: And if children, then heirs; heirs of God, and joint-heirs with Christ; if so be that we suffer with him, that we may be also glorified together."

This is our potential, this is our nature, this is our purpose in life. We must follow the Savior and discover the capacity within us. In the last two verses of the hymn "Come Follow Me," we are charged:

> We must the onward path pursue
> As wider fields expand to view,
> And follow Him unceasingly,
> What'er our lot or sphere may be.
>
> For thrones, dominions, kingdoms, pow'rs
> And glory great and bliss are ours,
> If we, throughout eternity,
> Obey his words, "Come, follow me."
> (*Hymns*, no. 116, verses 5 and 6)

Our self-esteem takes us from a feeling of inner value to a progressive state, one where we are working at being our best selves. In this progressive condition we must stay positive in our pursuit to be an individual. As we desire to succeed, we can prepare ourselves for the challenges of life. We put effort into those things we want to accomplish. But opposition does not go away even when people have self-esteem. So we must be strong and powerful as we explore our potential and discover who we are. I would like to share a poem I wrote that summarizes my feelings about these principles.

> A personal view,
> The impression is you,
> The one who you really are.
> Improves beyond
> the standard ol' song;
> Content, yet progressive so far.

Both happy and sad,
both good and bad,
yet positive still the same.
With capable hands
as the Lord demands
prepared, no others to blame.

As bruised as I am,
still a powerful man
to crush the one I abhor.
The potential is there,
so Satan beware;
I am His, therefore I'll conquer.

—Michael Weir Allred

Chapter Five

You Can Handle Pressure!

When high school football, wrestling, and the school play were over, I had nothing to do after school anymore. So I would come home and watch "Gilligan's Island," one of the more intellectual programs from my era.

One afternoon, as I vegged out in my bedroom watching a black-and-white episode of "Gilligan's Island," I started getting a little hungry. I walked down into the kitchen and looked in the fridge, leaving the door wide open—you know the kind of thing that makes parents real mad—and I spotted some semi-appetizing food. There were two pieces of link sausage covered in grease inside a small eight-inch skillet. We didn't have a microwave oven at the time, so I just put it on the stove and turned it to high (I was really hungry). Then I went back to watching *Gilligan's Island.* I must have been really into the program, because I forgot all about my hunger. Some time later I looked down the hallway and I could see the reflection of flames shining on the wall. It was a fire. I thought, uh oh, what could I do? It was not just a normal fire, it was a grease fire. I ran downstairs, where my mom was taking a shower. "Mom there's a fire!" I shouted.

Now she didn't know how big a fire it was, so she just said, "The fire extinguisher's over by the washing machine!" I ran to the machine, grabbed the extinguisher, and hustled back upstairs. The flame was only about eight inches around. But when I tried to put out the flame, there was so much pressure inside the extinguisher that the whole skillet went flying across the room. Grease and powder were splattered everywhere.

I turned around and my mom was standing next to me. She was dripping wet with a towel wrapped around her and looked more than a little upset.

"Mike," she said with disgust, "Mike, why didn't you just put a lid on it?" But I didn't know what to do. It had been a stressful situation, and I was under a lot of pressure. Now with a chance to think, the experience of a few years gone by, and my mom's wise, yet firm counsel, I have realized that there were other options. I could have put a lid on the skillet, or I could have put baking power on it. In fact, the flame was so small that I could probably have blown it out with a deep breath. But because of the pressure of not knowing what to do right at that instant, I overreacted.

Pressure is all around us. It is part of our everyday lives. But how can we learn to handle this ever-present pressure?

I want to share some ideas that are helpful in this fight against pressure. But first of all, I would like to share with you a poem I wrote for a high school assembly.

"UBU"

UBU and I'll be me.
This is what we ought to be,
'cause time will pass and you will see
mistakes were no catastrophe.

Whether you be boy or you be girl,
we all do things to make toes curl.
Your head begins to spin and swirl;
You feel so sick you want to hurl.

We all mess up, but who's to blame;
the pressure's on this teenage game.

To be a clone would be so lame;
so be unique and not the same.

Some set their goals, but not too far.
They shoot for nothing more than par.
They hide themselves and who they are,
but deep within they'll find a star.
Don't do the things you ought not to.
You'll be the one they're glad they knew.
Let's be ourselves, that's what we'll do.
So I'll be me and UBU.

There is a lot of pressure out there. But you know the Lord planned for opposition in all things. In 2 Nephi 2:11, we read that "there must be an opposition in all things." It is opposition that gives us the chance to prove ourselves and to prove that we are sons and daughters of God.

I have found that there are different types of pressures. First, we have *natural pressure;* second, *peer pressure;* third, *organized pressure;* fourth, *social pressure;* and fifth, something I call *practical pressure.*

NATURAL PRESSURE

There are natural pressures that take place like the little fire. Things just happen. There was just a little fire and a dumb decision. Everybody deals with natural pressures, and there's nothing you can do to get away from them.

I graduated from high school in 1979, the end of the long hair generation. I had long hair and used to wear bell-bottom pants. The pants had to drag to the floor behind you; you could sweep the floor and walk down the hall at the same time. These bell-bottom pants were really cool, and they were high-waisted—up on your waist as high as your belly button. There usually weren't any pockets in the front or else there might be really small ones that could only hold a dime or two. You had to reach in with one finger to get your coin out. At one time, the really cool ones had a seam that went up one leg, around your behind, and down the other leg; we called them "saddle backs." Today pants are totally opposite; kids wear them down below their hips and are lucky if the pants stay on.

Another style kids were wearing at that time was what we called a half shirt. Half shirts were what we wore underneath our shoulder pads. When we wore a netted jersey and a half shirt, it wasn't as hot, because our mid-section was exposed. Actually, it was to show those ripples. Now I have just one big ripple. Thank goodness I don't wear those half shirts anymore!

One night, I was fully decked out in my half shirt, my long hair, my bell-bottom pants dragging behind me, and thongs on my feet. (You got the picture? I was really in style.) My dad and I were watching TV and he said, "Mike, could you take this letter down to the Borens for me?" (Brother Boren lived down the street.)

I said, "Sure." So I went outside and started jogging down the street. Of course, with my thongs on, jogging made a sound of flip, flip, flip, flip. But then I started hearing flip, flip, jingle, jingle, flip, jingle, flip. I thought to myself, "What's that sound?" I turned around and there was this huge German Shepherd coming right after me.

"What do I do?" I asked myself. I needed a quick answer. What do you do with natural pressure? How do you handle it? I didn't know. So I started looking around for a car to jump on or a fence to jump, anything. I finally noticed a tree that forked right at the base of the tree. It divided into two trunks and grew up about eight feet before there was one branch. That was the only tree I could see that I thought I could actually get to. I hit the tree with my left arm, which spun me around the back of the tree and scraped my arm and back in the process. Then I started to shimmy up as fast as I could. I made it to the first branch, and I hung on and looked down. The dog was jumping up in the air trying to bite me, but he couldn't reach me. It was kind of a humbling experience. Here I was, a high school senior, thinking I was quite studly in my football half t-shirt, but there I was hanging in a tree like a scared raccoon. Then, to make things worse, an older man walked out of his house and the dog ran away! I thought, "Now was that fair?" There I was thinking I was so tough, and this older man, without even trying, had scared away the same dog that had just chased me up a tree.

That is an example of natural pressure. Natural pressure just happens. The dog chased me; there was nothing I could do about it.

PEER PRESSURE

I was at a party one time, a party with both boys and girls. One of my friends said, "Hey, you guys, I've got a great game we could play. Mike, come here. You stand up here in front of everybody, and I'll go down around the hallway. You do the shape of a famous statue, and I'll tell you what you look like."

I thought to myself, "Okay, I can do that." So there I was at the party, everybody looking at me. I stood up in front of everybody and did an impersonation of the Angel Moroni. Now, first of all, that's a little bit risky to do in front of your peers. But I acted like Angel Moroni, standing there like I had a trumpet to my mouth.

"Okay," I said, "what do I look like?" And he yells back from around the corner, "You look like a fool!" Well, he was right. And I really felt like a fool.

In Proverbs 12:15 we read, "The way of the fool is right in his own eyes." Now if my friend had said, "You look like Moroni," I probably would have laughed and said, "Man, how did you guess? That's unbelievable." But because he said I looked like a fool, I wanted to climb into a hole. That's the way peer pressure works.

This same friend, when we were fifteen years old, invited me to another party at his house. Now if there's a time in life that seems to be full of peer pressure, I believe it's when we're fifteen years old. The party was mostly guys from the varsity football team. At the high school I attended, we had varsity, junior varsity, and sophomore football teams. I was a sophomore. If there was a group of people that I wanted to impress, it had to be those senior boys on the varsity football team. That was because sometimes I had to practice with them, and if they liked you, you wouldn't get smashed.

So there we were at this party, and everything was going okay. Everybody was dancing, and I was just sitting there hanging out, enjoying myself. I wasn't even dancing with anybody, because all the girls had hooked up with the older, more mature boys who wore lettermen jackets and had a driver's license. So I was just watching the party.

Then a boy showed up with a paper sack. He set it down on the bar and pulled out a carton of orange juice, a package of clear plastic cups and a bottle of vodka. Then he mixed the drinks together and passed them around. Now here was one guy I was really impressed with. He was a linebacker and that was one of my positions. He came up to me and said, "Mike, can I fix you a drink?"

Now, what should I do? What do I say to these guys? Here I was a sophomore. They were seniors, and I wanted to impress them without hurting their feelings or getting them angry at me. I knew it would be risking my life if I were to condemn them, so what could I say? "Uh, my . . . my mom said I couldn't drink tonight." Or maybe I could have borne my testimony to them: "I know the Word of Wisdom is true." I didn't know what to do, so I said, "Uh, I'm in training."

Training? Why did I say that? Training for *what?* He was on the same team that I was. But he didn't laugh, and he didn't beat me up. He just said, "You know that's so cool. That's impressive that you stand up for what you believe in like that." Now you would think that would take the pressure off, but that's not what happened. In fact, it was just the opposite. Here was a neat guy, who was really well-liked, very successful, very athletic, going the opposite direction I was, and that created pressure for me. Now one of the reasons we sometimes don't learn to handle peer pressure is because we usually think of it as one person trying to get another person to do the same thing. But we can actually feel pressure when others go a different direction, because our minds start to think, "You mean I could be like them? I could drink and still be cool?" The guy that I wanted to impress didn't have to say, "Come on, have a drink." All he said was, "That's cool." But I still felt pressure. Even when others aren't trying to get us to do something, we can still feel peer pressure.

There was no way I was going to break the Word of Wisdom, but still the pressure was on. I didn't want to be different. The pressure got to me, so when nobody was looking, I walked over to the bar area, grabbed a clear cup, and poured a full glass of orange juice. The rest of the night I just carried it with me, playing like I was drinking. Why didn't I just stand up for what I believed in? Or why didn't I just leave? I walked around the party with this clear glass of orange juice, taking a sip once in a while, not wanting to drink too much or somebody would refill it. I stayed totally alert, with all my faculties about me, as I watched everybody else make fools of themselves. It was very sad.

Another sad part in all this is that for the rest of my high school career, the guys wouldn't believe me when I told them I never drank. They would say, "Oh, no way, man. At that one party you were so wasted, man." No, I wasn't. Even though I was determined not to drink, I still felt peer pressure. But that's the way peer pressure is.

ORGANIZED PRESSURE

To me, organized pressure is the worst. Let me explain what I'm talking about. Why does root beer have to come in a bottle that looks like a beer bottle? Why does beef jerky come in little containers that look like chewing tobacco? I call these "wannabes," because these containers give the appearance of being the "bad stuff." If a young person starts to take on the image—just as I did at the party—then he or she is more apt to actually go a step further. But if we avoid the very appearance of evil, we are that much further away from sin. Sin is progressive. If someone takes some beef jerky, sticks it in his lip, and walks around the school with his lip rolled out, the round container in his pocket, he's more likely to become involved in the actual thing later on. Satan understands how this concept works. Now the people who make these containers may not realize this concept, and I don't believe they have thought it through, but I do think Satan is more involved than we think. He knows exactly what he is doing.

On Tuesday, May 31, 1994, an Associated Press article said that the chiefs of the seven largest tobacco firms responded, under oath at a congressional hearing, that nicotine isn't addictive and there is no proof that smoking causes disease. On the 2nd of November, in 1994, my father passed away from heart failure and complications arising from cancer. My father smoked. Now you try to tell me that smoking doesn't cause disease. Even if Congress can't figure it out, the Lord knows. In Section 89 of the Doctrine and Covenants, he tells us why there is a Word of Wisdom problem. Verse 4 reads, "In consequence of the evils and designs that do and will exist in the hearts of conspiring men in the last days. . . ." Why is there a Word of Wisdom problem in the world today? Because of the hearts of conspiring men in the last days. These guys are always wondering how they can make money off of people and how they can get people addicted to a product that will then make them a lot of money.

The cigarette companies say they don't market to the youth. Well, here's just one example to contradict that. My son's favorite book has a pop-up alligator. As you open it up, the pop-up alligator takes a bite at you. One day, my son and I were sitting in the dentist's office, and he said, "Dad, look at this advertisement." It was an advertisement for Winston Select cigarettes. Like the book with the pop-out picture, the ad was an eagle and its wings flapped when you opened the page. Kids love that stuff. Now, can you see some fifty-year-old man saying, "Hey, honey, come here and check this baby out. I want you to run on down and get me some Winston Selects right now." I don't think so.

Consider this: ". . . approximately 5,000 people a day quit smoking, and another 1,000—-every single day—-die from cigarette smoking, or one in every ninety seconds, in the United States alone. This means that each day 6,000 people either kick the habit or kick the bucket. No wonder the cigarette companies spend billions to keep their unwitting customers buying their lethal wares" (Malcolm S. Jeppsen, in *Conference Report,* April 1990, 58; or *Ensign*, May 1990, 44).

Now if you're a businessman, you think about your market and ask yourself when your customer starts smoking. You figure out that people start smoking at fourteen and fifteen years old. You figure out how many you're losing, which equals how much money you're losing. You realize that every day you're losing too much. These conspiring men are businessmen and they realize that for them to break even, just to make the same amount of money they made yesterday, they need to get about five thousand teenagers to start smoking every day—just to break even. They're actually losing.

"Smoking is indeed becoming less and less popular as the heavy smokers one by one pass on. If an industrial accident killed everyone in the entire Salt Lake Valley, the nation would be horrified. That, however, is the scale of the annual tobacco disaster. One out of every six people that die in the United States dies as a result of smoking" (Malcolm S. Jeppsen, in *Conference Report,* April 1990, 59; or *Ensign*, May 1990, 45). That's how many people are affected by these conspiring men.

You may know people who say, "Mormons have too many rules. You have too many things that control you. The Church leaders decide what you'll do." When I was fifteen years old, I made certain choices such as "No, I won't drink," and "No, I won't smoke." At approximately the same time, a boy about my same age decided, "I can't be active in the Church because there are too many rules and too many restrictions." He started to smoke, drink, and take drugs. About five years ago, I was sitting in my seminary class teaching a lesson when a friend came into the back door and said, "Mike, can you go with me right now to the hospital?"

I said, "Why, what's wrong?"

He said, "My cousin's in the hospital. He's attempted suicide."

I said, "Sure, I can go with you. Let me get somebody to cover my class." On our way up to the hospital I asked what had happened. My friend told me that the night before his cousin had been drinking and smoking pot, and he put a gun in his mouth and shot himself. Now, this is the boy who wanted to be free and make his own choices. But now he is a quadriplegic living on life support. So, who is more free? The one who chooses to abstain from doing those type of things or the one who says "I can do what I want"?

The organized pressure that comes from the big businesses that promote tobacco and alcoholic beverages destroys many, many lives, but to them, that's just business as usual.

SOCIAL PRESSURE

I heard about a technique for catching monkeys that I thought was hilarious. When someone wants to catch a monkey, he finds out where there's a bunch of monkeys and rolls out a barrel of wine. He opens it up and then leaves. Pretty soon, one of the monkeys comes down because he's curious and he gets into the wine. He drinks a little bit, starts to drink a little more, and then he lets out a scream. All the other monkeys come and gather around and start drinking the wine. Soon you've got a bunch of drunk monkeys, and all the monkey-catcher has to do is walk over, grab one of the monkeys by the hand, and start walking down the trail. Soon all the monkeys start holding hands and the man just leads them down the trail *(see Stories for Mormons,* selected and edited by Rick Walton and Fern Oviatt [Salt Lake City: Bookcraft, 1983] p. 119).

People aren't all that different from monkeys. In fact, not only have large groups of people been taken into bondage but whole civilizations have fallen because people chose to follow a wrong idea. For example, in 1 Samuel chapter 8, the children of Israel tell the prophet Samuel that they want a king, because they want to be like the other nations. Why did they want a king? It appears that they, as a society, were feeling some pressure to conform, to be like other people. But Mosiah explains in the Book of Mormon why it's not always a good idea to have a king.

> If it were possible that you could have just men to be your kings, who would establish the laws of God, and judge this people according to his commandments, yea, if you could have men for your kings who would do even as my father Benjamin did for this people–I say unto you, if this could always be the case then it would be expedient that ye should always have kings to rule over you. . . .
>
> [But] because all men are not just it is not expedient that ye should have a king. . . .
>
> For behold, how much iniquity doth one wicked king cause to be committed, yea, and what great destruction! (Mosiah 29:13, 16-17)

Whole societies of people have been completely destroyed because they were influenced to live a life of sin by unrighteous leaders.

Just because it's popular or everybody does it, doesn't make it right. Abortion is very common today in the world, but it doesn't make it right. Lotteries are another example. Just because they're voted in by popular vote doesn't make them right. When the majority chooses evil, the society has started to fall.

When a teenager comes home from school and says, "But Mom, everybody's wearing them," he or she is feeling social pressure. But just because everybody's wearing a certain item of clothing, or living at a certain level that is just a little out of order with the Lord's standards, that doesn't make it right. We need to stay firm in His standards. Entire societies have fallen because one or two people did something wrong and somebody followed them.

PRACTICAL PRESSURE

Earlier I said that I would never drink. I'd like to share with you a situation that convinced me to never drink. When I was a boy, probably between eight and ten years old, I was at my friend's house, playing down in his basement. We could hear his mom and dad upstairs yelling at each other. We didn't know what was going on, but we knew his dad was drunk. We went outside as the dad came out the door with a chair in one hand and a rope in the other. And while everyone was yelling at each other, the dad walked out underneath the family tree in the back yard and he hung himself while I was there. To a little boy that was a serious object lesson. If that was what alcohol did to a person, I didn't want to have any part of it. If it could mess up my friend's family like that, I didn't want it. Even though my friend's father was rescued by his family, they couldn't control his every move. I don't remember how many months or years later it happened, but he did finally kill himself when he was drunk. And if that's what alcohol does to somebody, I wanted to stay away from it.

We can overcome these negatives types of pressure, and we can do this using what I call practical pressure.

Number one,

Learn from other people's mistakes. Don't try it on your own. You don't have to learn through your own mistakes. I didn't have to become an alcoholic to see if that was the life I wanted to live. I learned from another's mistake and that became a great blessing in my life.

Number two,

Take the pain up front. At a fireside I attended in Idaho, Vaughn J. Featherstone gave this advice. He said, "Take the pain up front." Take the pain now. Don't wait. Don't get involved and say okay, I'll do this and this and then I'll stop. As we commit sin it becomes too difficult to get out. We lose the desire to be good because the Spirit has withdrawn. We can take the pain right now, up front, by saying, "No, I won't do this or I won't do that even though others might laugh at me or think I'm strange." Here are some comebacks that might help take the pain up front:

Someone says, "Hey, how about a beer?"
You say, "No thanks, I'm in the next Boston Marathon."
Or you could say, "No, I'd rather have some sushi."
Or, "No, I'm allergic to that."
Or, "I'd break out in a bad rash."
Or, "No, thanks. Could I have a pop instead?"
"No, thanks. I like mornings."
"I'd be grounded for life."
"My parents would kill me."
"And I thought you were my friend."

Or someone says, "How about a cigarette?"
"No, thanks. I like my lungs."
"Have you ever kissed somebody who smokes? YUCK!"
"Let's go inhale my exhaust first."
"You're too cute to smoke."
"Have you heard the latest statistics about smoking?"
"I enjoy my life. Why cut it short?"
"My doctor said I can't. You know, medical reasons."
"Boy, you should read Brother Allred's book."
Or "No, thanks, someone I know died from smoking."
Or "If the Lord had wanted us to smoke, he would have put smokestacks on our heads."
Or just say, "NO!"

For sexual advances, you might try one of the following:
"Have you ever heard of scarlet fever?"
"Did you know my Dad's a karate expert?"

"I've gotta go prepare my talk on the law of chastity."
"My body is a temple. It's not a visitor's center."
"My body's a temple and you don't have a recommend."
"Let me tell you about the three degrees of glory."
"Have you ever worried about the AIDS epidemic?"
"Take me home and I'll give you a kiss good-bye."
"I love my future children too much."
In other words, you can just say "NO!"

Sure, it might hurt a little bit, but it's not going to hurt as badly now as the other more serious problems would later. Take the pain up front.

Number three,

Remember to have a positive attitude. Charles Dudley Warner said, "The winds of life can move you along or hold you back. It all depends on how you set your sail." A sailboat only sails if there's pressure. A balloon looks better as long as there's pressure inside. A kite flies higher when there's pressure blowing against it. It's our attitude towards the pressure that becomes the catalyst to make us like our Father in Heaven.

Number four,

Don't add to the pressure. Don't create your own pressure and help Satan tempt you more. Sometimes we are actually putting more pressure on ourselves when we think everybody is doing this or that, and we're different if we don't. That's one of Satan's many lies: "You're different and if you're not doing it like everybody else, you're missing out." Don't add more pressure than what's already there. Don't use phrases like "it's only natural" or "everybody wears them." Don't put it on yourself. Realize what's going on. In 1 Corinthians 10:13 we read, "There hath no temptation taken you but such as is common to man; but God is faithful, who will not suffer you to be tempted above that ye are able; but will with the temptation also make a way to escape, that ye may be able to bear it." While you're finding the way to escape, don't add more to the temptation.

Number five,

Come unto the Savior. Elder Vaughn J. Featherstone shared a little poem with our seminary faculty in Shelley, Idaho. He said we would never forget it, and I never have, and I always like to share it with people, because it has a great message.

> Humpty Dumpty sat on a wall.
> Humpty Dumpty had a great fall.
> All the king's horses and all the king's men
> couldn't put Humpty together again.
> But the King could.

Remember, if you've fallen in the past—if you've ever fallen and felt there was no way of getting out, the King can put you back together. He is the person who has provided the way for us to escape. He says in Matthew 11:28, "Come unto me all ye that labor and are heavy laden, and I will give you rest," that sweet rest that comes only to those persons who are living in accordance with the will of the Lord and those who have fallen, but who come back to Him in repentance and actually have used the Atonement that has been provided for us.

Hymn number 105, "Master the Tempest is Raging," verse two says:

> Master, with anguish of spirit
> I bow in my grief today.
> The depths of my sad heart are troubled.
> Oh waken and save, I pray.
> Torrents of sin and of anguish
> Sweep o'er my sinking soul,
> And I perish! I perish! dear Master.
> O hasten and take control!"

An answer to this plea is given in Hymn number 85, "How Firm a Foundation," verses three through five and verse seven:

"Fear not, I am with thee; oh, be not dismayed,
For I am thy God and will still give thee aid.
I'll strengthen thee, help thee, and cause thee to stand,
Upheld by my righteous, omnipotent hand.

When through the deep waters I call thee to go,
The rivers of sorrow shall not thee o'erflow,
For I will be with thee, thy troubles to bless,
And sanctify to thee thy deepest distress.

When through fiery trials thy pathway shall lie,
My grace, all sufficient, shall be thy supply.
The flame shall not hurt thee; I only design
Thy dross to consume and thy gold to refine.

The soul that on Jesus hath leaned for repose
I will not, I cannot, desert to his foes;
That soul, though all hell should endeavor to shake,
I'll never, no never, no never forsake!

The Savior has invited us to come unto Him. He is the way to handle the pressure that will come up in our life. The natural pressure, the peer pressure, the organized pressure, the social pressure—all these things can be more easily handled if we first, learn from others' mistakes, second, take the pain up front, third, keep a positive attitude, fourth, don't add any more to what's already there, and fifth, come unto the Savior. He is the Son of God. The Atonement was given for all of us that we could be made perfect and be like Him, but it will take His grace to do it. I testify to this in His holy name.

Chapter Six

You Recycle
Your Conversion

It's hard to believe, isn't it? King David, the one who had so much faith that he conquered the more powerful Goliath, committed adultery and murder. How could it happen? How could someone so good do something so bad? If someone that strong could fall, what's going to guarantee that we will never fall? Of course, no one is perfect and we all make mistakes, but this seems to be a little more serious than a simple mistake.

What can we do to make sure nothing like this ever happens to us? As we look at 2 Samuel chapter 11, we might be able to get some clues. In verse 2, David sees a woman washing herself. At that point he should have turned away and starting singing a hymn! The verse also gives us a clue to how long he looked. The scripture tells us that "the woman was very beautiful to look upon." Well, if he looked long enough to see she was beautiful, he was looking too long. At this point, it was time for repentance. It was time to ask for forgiveness, but that is not what David did.

Instead, he went another step closer to a major sin by "enquiring after the woman." He could have also repented here but he didn't. He "sent messengers" after her. *Now* it was crucial to repent. *Now* was the time to change directions before it was too late. But David went a major step in the wrong direction and committed adultery. Why didn't he stop sooner? How could he have let this happen?

But even after committing this extremely serious sin, there was still the possibility of repentance. It would have been difficult, but the power of the atonement was still available. However, even at this point, he wasn't able to exercise the necessary faith to repent. He sought to hide his sin and when those efforts wouldn't work, he arranged for the death of the woman's husband.

WHY REPENT

If you take a cup and fill it full of water then drop in a few small rocks, the water spills over allowing room for the rocks. When we commit sin, it's like putting rocks in our life; those rocks push out the Spirit. When we sin, the Spirit has to withdraw. Elder Henry D. Moyle said, "With transgression we also lose the Spirit of God and the Holy Ghost as our comforter" *(Conference Report,* April 1963, p.46). When the Spirit withdraws, our lives become darkened. Elder Joseph Anderson added his witness to this principle when he said, "But when we fail to keep the Lord's commandments and wickedness prevails, darkness comes into our lives, and great is the darkness when the Spirit of the Lord withdraws from us" *(Ensign,* December 1971, p. 127). This is one of the consequences of sin. The Lord says, "For I the Lord cannot look upon sin with the least degree of allowance. . . . And he that repents not, from him shall be taken even the light which he has received" (D&C 1:31, 33).

With the loss of the Spirit, our ability to withstand temptations becomes weaker, and soon we find ourselves in jeopardy of committing more serious sin. President Spencer W. Kimball explained:

> As the transgressor moves deeper and deeper in
> his sin, and the error is entrenched more deeply and
> the will to change is weakened, it becomes increas-
> ingly near-hopeless, and he skids down and down

until either he does not want to climb back or he has lost the power to do so. (*The Miracle of Forgiveness*, p. 117)

Elder James E. Talmage added his concern for those who procrastinated the day of their repentance. He said, " As the time of repentance is procrastinated, the ability to repent grows weaker; neglect of opportunity in holy things develops inability" (*The Articles of Faith,* p. 114).

Perhaps that is why Amulek teaches us that if we procrastinate our repentance until death we "become subjected to the spirit of the devil . . . therefore, the spirit of the Lord hath withdrawn" (Alma 34:32-36).

Repentance means more than just taking the spiritual rocks out of our life; we must regain the Spirit we have lost. The rocks do need to be removed, but the cup needs to be filled up again with the Spirit of the Lord before Satan steps in and occupies the void. Like David, we should not wait to repent. We need to repent when we first notice a lack of the Spirit so we don't lose our ability to withstand the temptations of Satan. We need to ask ourselves what has caused the Spirit to withdraw? What in our lives can we improve on? Have we done anything that was offensive to God or that has caused the Savior to suffer?

HOW TO REPENT

Many people are confused about repentance. Often they fail to see the Savior involved in the process. We need to be assured that without the Savior there is no repentance process. James E. Talmage taught:

Repentance is a result of contrition of soul, which springs from a deep sense of humility, and this in turn is dependent upon the exercise of an abiding faith in God. Repentance therefore properly ranks as the second principle of the Gospel,

closely associated with and immediately following
faith. *(The Articles of Faith,* p. 109)

Elder Ronald E. Poelman said, "The beginning and completion of repentance leading to forgiveness is faith in Jesus Christ"
(Ensign, November 1993, p. 84). Whenever we discuss our
repentance, let us always remember who made it possible.
    Other common misconceptions are:
        Repentance is only for teenagers.
        Repentance is only for people who commit really
            bad sins.
        If I've confessed, I've repented.
        I've already confessed to the Lord. He can tell my
            bishop if He wants to.
        Just be patient. Time heals all wounds.
        I know I've been forgiven, but there is no way I
            can forgive myself or anyone else.
        Repentance is easy so I'm going to sin now and
            repent later.
        All I have to do is stop sinning, right?
        I'm not sure I can stay strong so I'll wait and
            repent later, just in case.
        Repentance causes too much pain and embarras-
            ment, and I don't want to go through it.
        Because I've sinned so badly, I'm useless and I'll
            never be worth anything.
    With all of the misconceptions about repentance, how do we
really repent?
    There are various lists of the basic steps for repentance, but
some are different than others. The doctrines are not different,
but the needed steps to be taken may vary. With this in mind,
Elder Neal A. Maxwell explained that real repentance is not a
mechanical checklist; each portion of repentance is essential,
often overlapping and reinforcing (see *Ensign,* November 1991,
p. 30). Many of our Church leaders have given excellent talks on

repentance that can help us better understand this process. President Spencer W. Kimball taught five steps to repentance (see *Ensign*, November 1980, pp. 97-98). Elder Robert D. Hales gave a wonderful talk wherein nine steps were implied (see *Conference Report*, October 1976, p. 34-36). Elder Hugh W. Pinnock described eight principles (see *Conference Report*, April 1982, p. 16-17). Elder William J. Critchlow, Jr., taught about the seven R's of repentance (see *Conference Report*, April 1962, p. 38-40). As a last example, Elder Ronald E. Poelman taught about eight complimentary steps (see Conference Report, October 1993, p. 113-15). Not all of these brethren provided steps for repentance in their talks, but they all shared principles for repentance.

After this discovery, I decided to make a list of all the overlapping steps and principles to see what I could find. I found that there was an overall consensus on three or four repentance steps but that, inclusively, there were ten total steps. The ten steps were:

1. Recognize the sin.
2. Experience Godly sorrow.
3. Confess.
4. Abandon and forsake the sin.
5. Forgive self and others.
6. Do God's will.
7. Make things right.
8. Build strength to resist.
9. Help others to repent.
10. Become an example of repentance.

What a great list—ten steps of repentance that include the fruits of repentance! These are wonderful principles that can guide anyone toward repentance, but how can we remember them?

While looking for an easy way to remember this process of repentance, I was one day searching the scriptures to find a reference that would walk us through these ten overlapping, complimentary principles of real repentance. During my search, the thought came to me that repentance is kind of like *recycling our conversion.* I later realized that the cycle of conversion is taught in the beatitudes, which are taught in Matthew 5 and 3 Nephi 12.

The Lord gave the beatitudes in the Sermon on the Mount, the greatest sermon ever taught by the greatest teacher who ever lived. The Savior delivered this same sermon to the Nephites during one of His visits to the American continent. He set up the presentation of the beatitudes with a priesthood leadership meeting wherein He declared His doctrine to His newly called servants. His doctrine is faith, repentance, baptism, and the gift of the Holy Ghost (see 3 Nephi 11:31-41).

As I contemplated the principles of the gospel and the beatitudes, I wondered, could the steps of repentance possibly be hidden in the beatitudes? I believe they can.

Blessed are:	They who:
the poor in spirit	recognize their sin
they that mourn	experience Godly sorrow
the meek,	confess
they who hunger and thirst after righteousness	abandon and forsake their sin
the merciful	forgive self and others
the pure in heart	do God's will
the peacemakers	make things right
they who are persecuted for righteousness sake	build strength to resist

Ye are the:	They who:
salt of the earth	help others to repent
light of the world	become an example of repentance

What a wonderful truth! As we continue to repent, we recycle our conversion. Elder Marion G. Romney explained it this way:

A testimony comes when the Holy Ghost gives the earnest seeker a witness of the truth. A moving testimony vitalizes faith; that is, it induces repentance and obedience to the commandments. Conversion, on the other hand, is the fruit of, or the reward for, repentance and obedience. (Of course one's testimony continues to increase as he is converted.) *(Conference Report,* October 1963, p. 24)

The Spirit gives us a testimony of truth, which induces repentance and obedience. The reward for our repentance and obedience is a conversion that continues to increase our testimony. Thus we see the recycle process occurring.

To further illustrate how this happens in our personal lives, let's look again at the beatitudes. Because "R" words are used most frequently in the repentance process, I will re-list these steps again below. I've also listed the steps under three categories: (1) Remove the sin, (2) Refill with the Spirit, and (3) Results of Repentance.

1. Remove the Sin

Recognize	Poor in Spirit	Recognize the sin
Remorse	Mourn	Feel Godly sorrow
Report	Meek	Confess
Resolve	Hunger & Thirst	Abandon and forsake sin

2. Refill with the Spirit

Reflect	Merciful	Forgive
Recommit	Pure in Heart	Do His will
Restore	Peacemakers	Make things right

3. Results of Repentance

Resilient	Persecuted	Gain strength to resist
Rescue	Salt	Help others
Radiate	Light	Become an example

Notice the way these principles compliment each other in the following step-by-step application.

You begin to come unto Christ when you:

> —*recognize*
>> a lack of His spirit in your life because you have offended the Spirit and caused it to withdraw, so you feel . . .
>
> —*remorse*
>> because this action has caused the Savior to suffer, requiring us to . . .
>
> —*report*
>> the problem to the Lord and His servants through prayer and confession as required, with a . . .
>
> —*resolve*
>> to always remember Him in order to retain or regain His spirit which will help us to . . .
>
> —*reflect*
>> on His love and mercy as we forgive ourselves and others and . . .
>
> —*recommit*
>> to obey Him in all things and lose the desire for sin, after which we will make . . .
>
> —*restitution*
>> making whole as the Prince of Peace requires, staying...
>
> —*resilient*
>> in our testimonies of Christ as we help. . .
>
> —*rescue*
>> his other children, who need joy, mercy, and salvation while constantly . . .
>
> —*radiating*
>> the Savior's light, which helps us and others to again . . .
>
> —*recognize* . . . as we begin the process once more.

BABY STEPS TO A LENGTHENED STRIDE

With the beatitudes, Christ taught the multitudes the steps that would help them through His doctrine. The beatitudes are progressive baby steps that will help us "lengthen our stride" (see *Teachings of Spencer W. Kimball,* p. 174). It must not be perceived that these steps are infantile or childish, but rather, that they are "line upon line" movements toward conversion and eventually perfection (see D&C 98:12).

STEP #1 Blessed Are the Poor in Spirit

During general conference, Franklin D. Richards taught that "*Blessed* means happy, favored and glorified" *(Ensign,* November 1983, p. 57). We are, without a doubt, blessed when our faith motivates us to repent. Repentance is part of a growing life and, while growing, there is always need for adjustment (see Hugh B. Brown, *Eternal Quest,* p. 99). Neal A. Maxwell said of repentance: "It is available to the gross sinner as well as to the already-good individual striving for incremental improvement. . . .There can be no repentance without recognition of the wrong" *(Ensign,* Nov 1991, p. 30).

We are in the process of improving when we recognize that we are lacking spiritually. Back in 1969, President Alvin R. Dyer was a counselor in the First Presidency when he explained:

> Repentance is a principle of eternal growth for the individual. . . . If a man has a desire in his heart to know the truth, the normal and positive reaction, as his faith expands, causes him to know that he has participated in volitional acts that are wrong and therefore sinful. In this respect, all are in need of repentance. *(Improvement Era,* December 1969, p. 38)

It is when we don't think we need to repent that we are in trouble. "If we say that we have no sin, we deceive ourselves, and the truth is not in us" (1 John 1:8).

David O. McKay said, "The first step to knowledge is a realization of the lack of it" *(Gospel Ideals,* pp. 12-13). So likewise the first step to spirituality is a realization that we are "poor in spirit."

STEP #2 Blessed Are They That Mourn

Once we have recognized our sin and have realized that we have caused the Savior to suffer, we begin to feel remorse. This important step was clearly explained by President Ezra Taft Benson who said:

> It is not uncommon to find men and women in the world who feel remorse for the things they do wrong. Sometimes this is because their actions cause them or loved ones great sorrow and misery. Sometimes their sorrow is caused because they are caught and punished for their actions. Such worldly feelings do not constitute "godly sorrow" (2 Corinthians 7:10).
>
> Godly sorrow is a gift of the Spirit. It is a deep realization that our actions have offended our Father and our God. It is the sharp and keen awareness that our behavior caused the Savior, he who knew no sin, even the greatest of all, to endure agony and suffering. Our sins caused him to bleed at every pore. This very real mental and spiritual anguish is what the scriptures refer to as having "a broken heart and a contrite spirit" (D&C 20:37). Such a spirit is the absolute prerequisite for true repentance. *(Teachings of Ezra Taft Benson,* p. 72)

We feel remorse because we have offended God and caused the Savior to suffer. Our suffering can motivate us to seek Christ's help and lead us back to His side. His suffering was to pay the price for our sins. In the words of Elder Ronald E. Poelman of the Seventy, "Throughout the repentance process we have feelings of regret, remorse, and guilt, which cause us to suffer. However, our individual suffering does not satisfy the demands of justice which follow disobedience to divine law. We cannot pay the price for our sins" *(Ensign,* November 1993, p. 85).

As we recognize our sin and experience remorse, we are truly blessed to mourn. This is because when we feel godly sorrow we are on our way back to Him.

STEP #3 Blessed Are the Meek

Meek people are submissive and humble. They are willing to do whatever their Heavenly Father wants them to do. For example, in Alma 22:18, the father of King Lamoni said he would give away all his sins to know God. Even though he was the king, he was demonstrating a very meek attitude. Elder Maxwell said if we were more meek, we would repent more regularly. He also explained, "True repentance also includes confession. . . . One with a broken heart will not hold back. As confession lets the sickening sin empty out, then the Spirit which withdrew returns to renew" *(Ensign,* November 1991, p. 31).

The scriptures teach us that we must confess our sins. In 1 John 1:9, we read, "If we confess our sins, [Christ] is faithful and just to forgive us our sins, and to cleanse us from all unrighteousness."

The instructions on confession from Elder Richard G. Scott are very clear:

> You always need to confess your sins to the Lord. If they are serious transgressions, such as immorality, they need to be confessed to a bishop or stake president. Please understand that confession is not repentance. It is an essential step, but is not of itself adequate. Partial confession by mentioning lesser mistakes will not help you resolve a more serious, undisclosed transgression. Essential to forgiveness is a willingness to fully disclose to the Lord and, where

necessary, [allow] His priesthood [to] judge *all* that you have done. *(Ensign,* May 1995, p. 76)

This step must not be avoided or the repentance process is not complete. The Bible tells us, "He that covereth his sins shall not prosper" (Proverbs 28:13). The person who is meek enough to report before the Lord and confess appropriately is most assuredly blessed.

STEP #4 Blessed Are They Which Do Hunger and Thirst After Righteousness

By this ye may know if a man repenteth of his sins—behold, he will confess them and forsake them" (D&C 58:43). As we abandon our sins we begin to turn away from the evil and turn toward righteousness. We leave the sin behind and become hungry for good. Our desire to become more like our Father in Heaven makes us "thirsty." Like our natural desire for food and water, repentance becomes a vital necessity to our craving soul. Richard G. Scott said the process of forsaking our sins "is an unyielding, permanent resolve to not repeat the transgression." He adds that "by keeping this commitment, the bitter aftertaste of that sin need not be experienced again" *(Ensign,* May 1995, p. 76). This resolve to never repeat the sin needs to be firm, for to the soul that repeats the sin shall the former sins return. (see D&C 82:7).

We are in a blessed state when we resolve to forsake our sins and begin to hunger and thirst for righteousness.

STEP # 5 Blessed Are the Merciful

One of the difficult principles in the process of repentance for us to live is that of forgiving ourselves and others. Dallin H. Oaks said, "Forgiveness is mortality's mirror image of the mercy of God" *(Conference Report,* October 1989, p. 81). We must learn to reflect the Savior's love and mercy. We must be willing to forgive all men as we have been commanded in Doctrine and

Covenants 64:10: "I the Lord will forgive whom I will forgive, but of you it is required to forgive all men."

Elder Neal A. Maxwell stated, "We can also be too unforgiving, refusing to reclassify others. . . . We cannot repent for someone else. But we can forgive someone else, refusing to hold hostage those whom the Lord seeks to set free!" *(Ensign,* November 1991, p. 32).

If this is where the true joy that the Savior experiences can be found, then we should do all we can to feel it and then reflect it. H. Burke Peterson said:

> The human soul seldom reaches such heights of strength or nobility as when it removes all resentments and forgives error or malice. No one can be classed as a true follower of the Savior who is not in the process of removing from his heart and mind every feeling of ill will, bitterness, hatred, envy, or jealousy toward another. *(Ensign,* November 1983, p. 60)

We need to make sure that we include ourselves in this reflection of the Savior's love and mercy so that we may be able to forgive ourselves as well as others and be blessed for reflecting His mercy, as we are in necessity of obtaining the same.

STEP #6 Blessed Are the Pure in Heart

It is true that the process of repentance changes our actions, but real repentance also changes our heart. Unless we have a pure heart, we cannot see God for no unclean thing can enter into the kingdom of heaven (see 1 Nephi 10:21). N. Eldon Tanner gave us this clear instruction when he said:

> How many of us are guilty of keeping the letter of the law and forgetting the spirit of the law? . . . Do we place more stress on an external act to be seen of

men than on a change of heart? The only way to cleanse the inside of the cup is to be pure in heart by being humble and turning from our evil ways and by living the gospel of Jesus Christ to the best of our ability. We may be able to deceive men, but we cannot deceive God. *(Improvement Era,* December 1970, p. 32)

As our motives become more Christlike, we begin to do what is right instinctively. Elder Richard G. Scott expressed, "Full obedience brings the complete power of the gospel into your life with strength to focus on the abandonment of specific sins. It includes things you might not initially consider part of repentance, such as attending meetings, paying tithing, giving service, and forgiving others" *(Ensign,* May 1995, p. 76).

The Doctrine and Covenants teaches us that the person who repents and keeps the commandments will be forgiven (see D&C 1:32). President Kimball explained,

> Repentance must involve an all-out total surrender to the program of the Lord. That transgressor is not fully repentant who neglects his tithing, misses his meeting, breaks the Sabbath, fails in his family prayers, does not sustain the authorities of the Church, breaks the Word of Wisdom, does not love the Lord nor his fellowmen. A reforming adulterer who drinks or curses is not repentant. The repenting burglar who has sex play is not ready for forgiveness. God cannot forgive unless the transgressor shows a true repentance which spreads to all areas of his life. *(Miracle of Forgiveness,* p. 203)

We must recommit ourselves to the will of the Lord and obey all His commandments. We are definitely blessed when we are pure in heart, for the time will come that we shall see Him.

STEP #7 Blessed Are the Peacemakers

No matter who starts a quarrel, the one who ends it is the one who apologizes. When we have hurt someone, we need to make things right. We need to restore the peace and make whole that which was wronged. Richard G. Scott taught, "You must restore as far as possible all that which is stolen, damaged, or defiled. Willing restitution is concrete evidence to the Lord that you are committed to do all you can to repent" *(Ensign,* May 1995, p. 76).

Neal A. Maxwell added, "Sometimes, however, restitution is not possible in real terms, such as when one contributed to another's loss of faith or virtue. Instead, subsequent example of righteousness provides a compensatory form of restitution" *(Ensign,* November 1991, p. 31).

The scriptures teach us that when we make restitution, we shall live (see Ezekiel 33:15-16). When we become peacemakers, we become more like the Prince of Peace.

STEP #8 Blessed Are You When Men Shall Persecute You

During the process of repentance, we make serious changes. Neal A. Maxwell said, "Repentance requires both turning away from evil and turning to God. . . . Full repentance involves a *180-degree turn,* and without looking back. . . .Thus, while we are turning away from evil but have not yet turned fully to God, we are especially vulnerable. Yet we must not give up" *(Ensign,* November 1991, p. 30).

Why is it when a person tries to change, other people pull him down? As we change our life toward being more righteous, we need to remain resilient in our new attitude. We must be willing to be ridiculed for overcoming our weaknesses and for becoming more like Christ. When we are persecuted for being righteous, that tells us we must be doing something right. What a great honor to be grouped with the prophets (see Matthew 5:12).

We cannot give up after making it this far. If the pressure is on, the Lord will always be there. He said; "Come unto me, all ye that labour and are heavy laden, and I will give you rest"

(Matthew 11:28). Let us remain resilient in our testimony as we are blessed for our commitment to His name.

STEP #9 Ye Are the Salt of the Earth

If conversion is the result of our repentance, then what is the result of this conversion? By definition, a conversion is a change from one form or function to another. To convert is to alter something for a more effective utilization (see *Webster's Seventh New Collegiate Dictionary*, p. 183). Elder William J. Critchlow Jr. said, "To earn [the Lord's] forgiveness one should go the extra mile, forsaking not only his sins but adding . . . devotion and service to prove his love for him. Such devotion and service constitutes reformation" *(Conference Report,* April 1962, p. 38). We become reformed into servants of the Lord, and as we become more holy, we become more used by the Lord (see "More Holiness Give Me," *Hymns,* no. 131).

Our new assignment is to now become the "salt of the earth" and rescue those who are in need of repentance. Doctrine and Covenants 88:81 says, "Behold, I sent you out to testify and warn the people, and it becometh every man who hath been warned to warn his neighbor."

As we have been taught so many times, salt adds flavor, it preserves, and it heals. As we feel the sweet joy of repentance, we desire for others to experience that wonderful flavor. As we are forgiven of our sins, we desire our fellowmen to be preserved from the jaws of hell. And, as we have been healed from our weaknesses, we would that all men may be healed of that awful sickness that leads to spiritual death. Let us remember the example of the sons of Mosiah: "Now they were desirous that salvation should be declared to every creature, for they could not bear that any human soul should perish; yea, even the very thoughts that any soul should endure endless torment did cause them to quake and tremble" (Mosiah 28:3).

May we, in reality, become the salt of the earth, that we may rescue the lives of our brothers and sisters who need to be blessed.

STEP #10 Ye Are the Light of the World

We are commanded to be perfect. But, "being mortal, and despite our resolve and efforts, we will continue to fall short of perfection" (Elder Ronald E. Poelman, *Ensign,* November 1993, p. 85). Heber J. Grant provided hope concerning this principle when he said:

> I do not believe that any man lives up to his ideals, but if we are striving, if we are working, if we are trying, to the best of our ability, to improve day by day, then we are in the line of our duty, If we are seeking to remedy our own defects, if we are so living that we can ask God for light, for knowledge, for intelligence, and above all, for His Spirit, that we may overcome our weaknesses, then, I can tell you, we are in the straight and narrow path that leads to life eternal. Then we need have no fear. *(Gospel Standards*, pp. 184-85)

Joseph Fielding Smith stated:

> Here is where we are taught these simple truths of the gospel of Jesus Christ, in this probationary state, to prepare us for that perfection. It is our duty to be better today than we were yesterday, and better tomorrow than we are today. Why? Because we are on that road, if we are keeping the commandments of the Lord, we are on that road to perfection, and that can only come through obedience and the desire in our hearts to overcome the world. *(Doctrines of Salvation*, vol.2, pp. 18-19)

Alvin R. Dyer said, "Repentance leads the way to many regenerations, without which the soul shall never reach perfection" *(Improvement Era,* December 1969, p. 38). As we progress one step at a time through repentance, the world notices our progress. Maybe they will see the light of Christ shine in our eyes. Maybe they will see His image in our countenance. Or, maybe they will just notice His light radiating from the way we continually desire to become more like Him as we recycle our conversion again. Never forget how we are blessed throughout the process of repentance, conversion, and perfection. Ezra Taft Benson said it this way, "We are far short of the goal he set for us, but we must never lose sight of it; nor must we forget that our great climb toward the light, toward perfection, would not be possible except for his teachings, his life, his death, and his resurrection" (Ensign, June 1971, p. 34).

May we live in such a way that we may retain His spirit as we live a life of faith, repentance, and obedience, so that we can imagine to ourselves hearing the voice of the Lord say: "Come unto me ye blessed, for behold, your works have been the works of righteousness" (Alma 5:16).

Chapter Seven

You Can Forgive Others

The day I left for my mission, I learned a great object lesson. I packed as much as I could into my three pieces of luggage—two suitcases and a carry-on (two of which came from the thrift store). Because my well-worn luggage was so stuffed, I didn't have room for the care package I'd received from a semi-supportive young lady (which included some mint chocolate rice crispy treats, nicely wrapped in aluminum foil). I'd also gone to the bank to get 100 pennies to give out to the Japanese kids (although for some crazy reason, I didn't keep them in the roll). Not having anyplace to put these extras, I put the pennies and the rice crispy treats in my raincoat, and then wore the raincoat. Not a bad idea—unless you're wearing a thick three-piece polyester suit in the middle of July. And to top it all off, our layovers were in Los Angeles and Honolulu—in July!

While changing flights in Los Angeles, we missionaries had to take all our luggage with us to the connecting flight. I don't recall why; I think it was to teach me a lesson. I jingled because of the pennies, my arms stuck out because of the treats in my overcoat, and I was sweating like a horse. I got searched for metal everywhere I went. My carry-on was busting at the seams as I carried the other two pieces in each hand. Finally, to make things really interesting, the strap broke on my carry-on so I had to drag it behind me down the corridor. I was totally overloaded. I could not have carried one more thing with me.

Many of us try to go through life with extra heavy cargo. We have picked up a lot of baggage on the way, and we can't leave it behind. How do we know if we are carrying unnecessary cargo? Just ask yourself these questions:

Are you ever happy when something bad happens to someone who has offended you?

Do you wish you could get even?

Is there anyone you avoid who offended you?

When you get angry do you sulk for a few days?

Do you talk unkindly about those who offended you?

Do you frequently bring up past offenses?

Do you ever say, "I'll forgive, but I'll never forget"?

If you answered yes to any of these questions, you probably have a problem with being able to forgive. The media and the world often glamorize revenge, making it difficult for us to realize the need to forgive. If you have a problem with forgiving others, you are carrying around extra baggage.

WHY FORGIVE?
Resentment Harms You.

In Doctrine and Covenants 101:50 we read, "And while they were at variance one with another they became very slothful. . . ." When we bicker and argue, we can't get anything done— except the work of the devil. As far as spiritual progress goes, we are stuck.

When I was about five years old, my brother was helping my mom do laundry. We had an old washing machine with a wringer on top. My mom had let my brother feed the socks through the wringer, so of course I wanted to help. She handed me a sock and started to walk away. As I was feeding the sock through the wringer, I wasn't paying attention. Mom was out of the room and ready to go upstairs when my fingers got caught. Slowly the wringer started to pull all my fingers in. I started screaming for my mom, but she thought that my brother and I were fighting again, and in order to get us to stop, she turned off the light and continued to climb the stairs. My thumb had been pulled backward and my skin was torn open between my thumb and finger. My brother was trying to locate the release lever so I could remove my arm, but it was dark and he could not see. Finally, about the time my arm had gone all the way in, my brother found the controls and put the wringer in reverse. My arm had to go all the way through again.

Ultimately, my hand needed stitches, and my arm was put in a cast. Now, I have a few questions. Would it do me any good to hold a grudge against the washing machine? After all, I was the one who had been hurt. Or, if I had continued to hold onto the machine, would that have helped me at all? I could have kicked the washing machine, I could have called it names, I could have told everyone what a bad machine it was. But I did not have the time or energy to waste. I needed to be released so I could get some help. As long as I was stuck, I was still being hurt. Not until I was released did I get the help I needed.

It is the same with forgiveness. We need to be released from the hold of the hurt, so we can begin healing. When we can't forgive, we are only hurting ourselves.

Dallin H. Oaks said, "Modern saints know that one who subdues his own spirit is just as much a pioneer as one who conquers a continent" *(Conference Report,* October 1989, p. 81).

We Are Required to Forgive All.

When we feast upon the words of Christ, we can learn all things that we should do (see 2 Nephi 32:3). In Doctrine and Covenants 64:10, we read the Lord's directive about forgiving others: "I, the Lord, will forgive whom I will forgive, but of you it is required to forgive all men." Well, that seems simple enough. But how often do we have to forgive? Again the words of Christ have the answer: "Then came Peter to him, and said, Lord, how oft shall my brother sin against me, and I forgive him? till seven times? Jesus saith unto him, I say not unto thee,

Until seven times: but, Until seventy times seven" (Matthew 18:21-22). Jesus was not telling Peter to forgive four hundred and ninety times, but to *completely* forgive. We must always forgive because we have been commanded to forgive all men.

In describing the power of forgiveness, Bishop H. Burke Peterson said: "[Sin] has the power to drag people to the depths of hell; yet, when released from its hold, they may soar to celestial heights" *(Ensign,* November 1983, p. 59).

Remember You've Been Forgiven.

Because we have been forgiven, it is our responsibility to forgive others. But sometimes we forget that we have been given a great gift, and we refuse to share it with others. In Matthew, chapter 18, the Lord teaches that great parable about forgiving others. The Lord said:

> Therefore is the kingdom of heaven likened unto a certain king, which would take account of his servants.
>
> And when he had begun to reckon, one was brought unto him, which owed him ten thousand talents [the equivalent of hundreds of millions of dollars].
>
> But forasmuch as he had not to pay, his lord commanded him to be sold, and his wife, and children, and all that he had, and payment to be made.
>
> The servant therefore fell down, and worshipped him, saying, Lord, have patience with me, and I will pay thee all.
>
> Then the lord of that servant was moved with compassion, and loosed him, and forgave him the debt.
>
> But the same servant went out, and found one of his fellow servants, which owed him an hundred pence [three month's wages for a poor working

man]: and he laid hands on him, and took him by the throat, saying, Pay me that thou owest.

And his fellow servant fell down at his feet, and besought him, saying, Have patience with me, and I will pay thee all.

And he would not: but went and cast him into prison, till he should pay the debt.

So when his fellow servants saw what was done, they were very sorry, and came and told unto their lord all that was done.

Then his lord, after that he had called him, said unto him, O thou wicked servant, I forgave thee all that debt, because thou desirest me:

Shouldest not thou also have had compassion on thy fellow servant, even as I had pity on thee?

And his lord was wroth, and delivered him to the tormentors, till he should pay all that was due unto him.

So likewise shall my heavenly Father do also unto you, if ye from your hearts forgive not every one his brother their trespasses. (Matthew 18:23-35)

In another example, we read how Laman and Lemuel were cruel to Nephi. They beat him and tied him up, but Nephi frankly forgave them for all they had done to him (see 1 Nephi 7:21).

When we don't forgive, it is like walking backwards and keeping our eyes on the past while at the same time trying to move forward.

HOW TO FORGIVE:
Pray for Help.

Bishop H. Burke Peterson persuaded us to plead with the Lord for the power to forgive. He said, "Now, brothers and sisters, let us go to our homes and dismiss from our beings—and purge from our souls—the venom of any feeling of ill will or bitterness toward anyone. Let us strike from our hearts the unwillingness to forgive and forget; and, instead, approach men in the spirit of the Master. . . . Let us pray—rather, let us plead for the spirit of forgiveness" *(Ensign,* November 1983, p. 60).

Think of the Savior.

Isaiah chapter 43 has some great advice about learning to forgive. It says,

> Remember ye not the former things, neither consider the things of old. . . .
> I, even I, am he that blotteth out thy transgressions for mine own sake, and will not remember thy sins.
> Put me in remembrance: let us plead together: declare thou, that thou mayest be justified. (Isaiah 43:18, 25-26)

President Kimball counseled us to blot the memory from our minds. He taught,

> If we have been wronged or injured, forgiveness means to blot it completely from our minds. To forgive and forget is an ageless counsel. "To be wronged or robbed," said the Chinese philosopher Confucius, "is nothing unless you continue to remember it." (President Spencer W. Kimball, *Ensign,* November 1977, p. 48)

If we continue to remember our neighbor's trespasses, we are still being injured. Elder Eldred G. Smith told members at a general conference in 1961, "We must be willing to forgive and forget. Most of us have a natural ability to forget, especially the things we are supposed to remember. Most of us work diligently to increase our power to remember. However, in forgiving, we should increase or attempt to increase and work diligently to increase our power to forget" *(Conference Report,* April 1961, p. 68).

Speak Kindly of Those Who Have Offended You.

"Cease to contend one with another; cease to speak evil one of another" (D&C 136:23).

Remember our mothers' counsel: "If you can't say something nice, don't say anything at all"? A friend of mine who had been offended told me that even after she had forgiven her offender, other people she had told the situation to kept bringing it up and reminding her of her former ill feelings. It made it more difficult for my friend to get on with life and forgive and forget.

Pray for Those Who Have Offended You.

While sitting in my office early one morning, a young lady came in crying. She was very upset. She had a difficult time talking. I invited her to come in and sit down. As time passed, we were able to talk about the problem.

She said, "Brother Allred, what should I do? My dad yelled at me all the way to school, and I didn't do anything wrong."

I said, "What was he yelling about?"

"Everything!"

After a while, I became curious about her father.

I asked, "Is your father a Mormon?" She said no.

I asked her where he worked. She said, "He got laid off about five months ago and he has been trying to find a job, but things aren't going well for him."

I then asked her if there was a possibility that her dad was just upset and needed someone to unload on. Sometimes people are mad and we just happen to be around. Sometimes all we can do is to learn to stay out of their problems so that we can be there for them. This allows us to help *rescue* them in their time of need instead of making their time of need, *our* time of need. In this way, it becomes our opportunity to share charity and love.

To illustrate this principle, I would like to share an experience of Elder Marion D. Hanks:

> One afternoon about sunset [Elder Hanks] was traveling east on North Temple. As he approached the intersection of Main Street at North Temple, there was a car stopped at the traffic light. As he pulled up behind the car, his foot slipped from the brake and hit the accelerator, and he hit the car. Well, he was very embarrassed about it and was about to get out of his car when there emerged from the automobile a mountain, a giant of a man. "So," he said, "I stayed in my own automobile. The next five minutes I received the most vulgar, the most vile, the most wicked tongue lashing I have ever received in my life. After he was through mauling me verbally, he got back in his automobile and sped away. . . ."
>
> About two or three weeks later, Elder Hanks was at a stake conference in the Salt Lake Valley. Seated on the stand, he was looking down at the congregation. Lo and behold, there was his vulgar vile friend. Well, after the stake conference this good brother came up to the stand and asked Elder Hanks if he could have a few words with him. They went into another room, just the two of them, and this good brother apologized, asked for Elder Hanks to forgive him. He said, "Do you know, two or three weeks ago there on the street I made this great scene. I'm very sorry and very embarrassed, and I apologize for the language I used and the embarrassment I caused you. But you know, I was sitting in my automobile, waiting for the light to change and contemplating the events that had just transpired in my life in the past hour or so. I was on the way

home from the hospital to tell our four small children that their dear mother and my beloved wife and sweetheart had just passed away. My entire world had just caved in, and I was sitting there contemplating all of these things—the gloom and despair of my life—when you hit into the back of my car. So I ask for your forgiveness."

. . . Elder Hanks explained later, "I had made a man an offender for a word. On the basis of a few moments' exposure or experience with this man I had literally condemned him. . . ." (Max L. Pinegar, "The Weightier Matters of the Law," *Speeches of the Year 1975*, pp. 455-56)

In the Sermon on the Mount, the Savior taught, "Love your enemies, bless them that curse you, do good to them that hate you, and pray for them which despitefully use you, and persecute you; That ye may be the children of you Father which is in heaven" (Matthew 5:44-45).

Release Responsibility.

There is a difference between the words "tolerate" and "tolerant". We are taught to be a *tolerant* people, but we do not have to *tolerate* mistreatment. The Savior was a perfect example of the difference between these two terms. In Luke 23:34, we see an incredible example of tolerance. While hanging on the cross, our Savior pleaded with our Heavenly Father to forgive the soldiers who had crucified Him saying, "Forgive them; for they know not what they do." On the other hand, in Luke 19:45, we are shown an example of not tolerating inappropriate behavior. When the Savior entered the temple and saw that the money changers and sellers of animals had made it a "den of thieves." He could not tolerate it and cast them out, thus cleansing the temple for its proper use. He allowed the money changers to take responsibility for their own actions. He could then forgive them if they repented. That is tolerance. But He would not allow them to do wrong in the temple; that is, he would not tolerate their unrepentant wrongdoing.

Let us earnestly sing from the hymn "In Humility, Our Savior": "Fill our hearts with sweet forgiving; teach us tolerance and love" (*Hymns*, no., 172).

Trust in the Lord.

The Lord has the power to forgive, and he made the promise to forget our sins. But when we are the transgressor, are we supposed to forget? Marion D. Hanks said, "Almighty God has promised to forgive, and forget, and never mention the sins of which we have truly repented. But he has given us the gift of remorse to help us remember them constructively, thankfully, and humbly. . ." *(Ensign,* May 1979, p. 76).

Sometimes when someone has done something very wrong, it is difficult for us to see how we can ever forgive and forget. Sometimes it seems so wrong that we can't see how even the Lord can forgive and forget. And sometimes we are the one who has committed those terrible wrongs. At times like these, we must have faith in the Atonement. We must trust in the Lord. "Trust in the Lord with all thine heart; and lean not unto thine own understanding" (Proverbs 3:5).

In Doctrine and Covenants 64:11 we read, "And ye ought to say in your hearts—let God judge between me and thee, and reward thee according to thy deeds." Christ paid the price so that we can say, "The price for that sin has already been paid by Him in Gethsemane. I have no right to hold on to it and demand justice, so I gladly hand it back to Him and rejoice in His love and mercy" (Dallin H. Oaks, *Conference Report,* October 1989, p. 81).

Many of us try to go through life with extra heavy baggage. We have picked it up along the way, and we can't leave it behind. The Lord has said, "Come unto me, all ye that labour and are heavy laden, and I will give you rest" (Matthew 11:28).

He has already paid the price and suffered for our burdens. Let us exercise faith in the Atonement and lighten our load.

Chapter Eight

The Spirit Is Your Image Consultant

I couldn't believe it. I had a square bald spot cut in my hair just above my ear.

I had told my wife that the way to make a tapered haircut was to hold the buzzers next to the skin and then, as the razor moved up, to gradually move it away from my head. I didn't know if that was the right way, but it made sense to me. The only problem was that she forgot to move the razor gradually away as she moved it up. When she saw what had happened, she laughed so hard she fell to the floor. We called my sister-in-law, who is a beautician, and asked for help. It was difficult for her to help because she too fell on the floor laughing. Finally, I had to settle for a similar cut on the other side of my head.

So here I was, two square bald spots, one on each side of my head, and I had to return to teach my seminary class on Monday. Have you ever been teased in school about something you are wearing, or the way your hair looked? Can you imagine my fear? Can you feel my pain?

Actually, the students were very compassionate. Not only were they kind in not making fun of me, but one of the boys even said it was the "baddest" haircut he had ever seen.

If I had purposely chosen that haircut, you could probably tell a little bit about my personality. However, that's part of the problem—you can't always judge a book by its cover. But what's on the inside does seem to show up on the outside.

I want to make two points clear. First, I am not trying to present ideas on how to judge others. Second, people do judge us, so we need to be careful to stand as a witness for Christ in all things, and in all ways, and in all places. We can find out whether we are standing as witnesses by asking ourselves four questions:

Have you received His image in your countenance?

Does the light of Christ shine in your eyes?

Does the Father know His child?

Have you experienced a mighty change of heart?

Have You Received His Image in Your Countenance?

At general conference in October 1969, President David O. McKay recited this poem by an unidentified author (I've updated two lines to make them fit the 90s):

> You tell on yourself by the friends you seek,
> By the very manner in which you speak,
> By the way you employ your leisure time,
> By the use you make of dollar and dime.
> You tell what you are by the things you wear,
> And even by the way you wear your hair,
> By the way you laugh and the jokes you know,
> By the music you play on your stereo.
> You tell what you are by the way you walk,
> By the things of which you delight to talk,
> By the manner in which you bury deceit,
> By so simple a thing as how you eat.
> By the books you choose from the well-filled shelf.
> In these ways and more you tell on yourself.
> (*Improvement Era,* December 1969, p. 87)

Even in Old Testament times, those who participated in evil usually marked themselves. They would identify themselves with hair styles or by cutting or printing in their flesh (see us 19:27-28; 1 Kings 18:28). This doesn't sound just like ancient times, though, does it? It sounds like MTV. What goes on the inside shows up on the outside.

With all the stereotypical images in the world today, we should do some analysis as to which one helps the Lord. Even if the missionary is a cowboy from Montana—even if the missionary was the best skater in Seattle—the need is the same: When we are on the Lord's business we need to look the part in the eyes of those we are serving. We are actually taking on society's stereotypical appearance of a servant of the Lord. In the April general conference of 1973, President Harold B. Lee said:

> Priesthood is the power by which Heavenly Father works through men, through deacons, through teachers, through priests. . . . They would always want to appear at their best when they are exercising their priesthood. Their hair would be properly groomed; their clothing and appearance would reflect the sanctity they should feel in the performance of their priesthood duties. ("Follow the Leadership of the Church," *Ensign*, July 1973, p. 98)

I feel that this advice is equally important for the daughters of Zion. Both the young men and the young women who are trying to witness for the Lord need to ask themselves this serious question: Have you received His image in your countenance?

Does the Light of Christ Shine in Your Eyes?
The scriptures warn us of wolves in sheep's clothing. Some of the most infamous killers of our day have looked like nice people. Jeffery Dahmer and Ted Bundy were both successful in their evil, partly because of their appearance. 1 Samuel 16:7 tells us that man looks on the outward appearance, but the Lord looks on the heart. Do our actions equal our appearance?

As missionaries in Japan, my companion and I were once asked why we were so light. We semi-sarcastically answered that

it was because we were Caucasian. What the person was refer-
ring to, however, was more than an outward appearance. She
had seen something in us that was a result of our actions.

Look at the daily routine of missionaries. They start with
morning prayer and personal scripture study, and they avoid the
things of the world. Here seems to lie the key to the light of
Christ shining in our eyes. In 2 Nephi 32:3, we are told to feast
upon the words of Christ, and that the words of Christ, will
show us all things that we should do. In this way the Spirit
becomes our image consultant.

While growing up in the sixties and seventies, I had long hair. It
was really cool, I thought. If a parent or leader asked me to cut it,
I would use the familiar statement about the Savior having long
hair. I had a testimony of the gospel; and I believed the Church
was true. I really didn't see the need for a shorter hair cut.

Then one day my brother-in-law asked me if I had read the
Book of Mormon. I said I knew it was true without reading it.
He asked if I had a testimony of Joseph Smith. I said I did. He
then invited me to read the Book of Mormon, because Joseph
Smith said it was the keystone of our religion.

One of the reasons, why I had not yet read the Book of
Mormon was in the past. When I graduated from Primary, I was
presented with my own copy of the Book of Mormon. I took it
home that night and read and read. I'm sure I read at least two
chapters. I was feeling so spiritual that I even prayed as Moroni
did in the famous painting. I knelt down and put my folded
hands on top of my new Book of Mormon.

While I slept I had a really scary dream. I dreamt that I was in
a large white house going up a staircase. At the top of the stairs
was the traditional picture of the Savior. As I approached the
picture it turned and snarled at me. I ran down the stairs and
went to the local laundromat. Why the laundromat? I have no
clue. I was so scared that I woke up. Out of fear, I stopped
reading the Book of Mormon. It's hard to believe I let Satan
influence me like that.

While I was in ninth grade seminary, my teacher was sharing the warm feeling that we get from reading the Book of Mormon. I raised my hand and disagreed. He then put his hand on my shoulder and said to me, "He succeeded, didn't he? Satan tried to scare you away from reading the Book of Mormon." I then determined that I would not let Satan beat me again. By this time I wasn't much into reading. So here I was with my brother-in-law, deciding to read the Book of Mormon from cover to cover.

My job at that time was in downtown Indianapolis, to which I took the bus to work every day. I would read on my way there and on my way home. I read to midway through Alma before the messages really started to stick. I was reading about a great man named Ammon. Ammon was like an Arnold Schwarzeneggar with a testimony. By this time, instead of reading words I would start seeing the situations; I began visualizing what was happening. This visualization continued until I had completed the entire book. On the final day, when I was reading about the destruction of the Nephite people, I could hardly believe what had happened to them. So there I was, sitting on a crowded bus with tears in my eyes, because of the destruction of a people I had never met but had grown to love. I was hoping that the people sitting around me would think I had hay fever.

When I returned home and found the house empty, I knelt down and asked the Lord for another witness. I received my answer. I had already believed the Book of Mormon was true, but now I had read it. I learned to love the book during this time. My testimony was set on fire.

During this period I was sharing the gospel with my nonmember friend. Having had the experience in reading the Book of Mormon, I was now able to share some of my excitement with him. Soon, my friend too felt the Spirit and wanted to be baptized. And he wanted me to do the honors. It was just before his baptism that I approached my sister and asked her to cut my hair. Why was I choosing to cut my hair now? What about the statement about the Savior having long hair? Wasn't it okay to have hair like that and perform a baptism? While these thoughts went through my mind, I felt that the Spirit was telling me something. It is hard to use the excuse about the Savior having long hair when it is He who is telling you to cut it. The words of Christ were not only having an effect on my outward appearance, but also were having a still greater effect on my heart. To find out how your heart is doing, answer this question: Does the light of Christ shine in your eyes?

Does the Father Know His Child?

Have you ever been told to ask yourself, "What would Jesus do?" I think this is great advice, but I would like to add one more part.

When I was ten to twelve years old, my little nephew had been hurt and his mother thought he had a concussion. She called my mother and asked us to go get them and take them to the hospital. While we were at their house, my mother went inside with my sister and my nephew and left me alone in the car.

What would Jesus do? I loved this nephew very much and I didn't want him to be hurt. So I knelt down on the floor and prayed to my Heavenly Father that he wouldn't have a concussion. He was too little; if someone should have to have a concussion, it should be me. Is that what Jesus would do?

When we arrived at the hospital, to our joy my nephew did not have a concussion. The Lord had answered my prayer. In fact, He answered in every detail, because not long after that I fell in a shower and got a concussion. If I were to say that same prayer today, I would leave out that little part about *my* getting the concussion.

Not only should we ask what Jesus would do, but we should also ask why? Why would the Savior go to church? Why would the Savior obey the Word of Wisdom? Why would the Savior study the scriptures every day? There are three main reasons why people do good: fear, pride, and love. The Savior's motivation is always love. When we begin to do *right,* we are going in the *right* direction. When we begin to do the *right* things for the *right* reasons, then we are *right*eous. At general conference in October 1986, Elder Neal A. Maxwell said: "We cannot share in his power without sharing in his attributes. . . . We cannot reenter his house until our behavior would let us feel at home." ("God Will Yet Reveal," *Ensign,* November 1980, p. 54). When it is time for us to come home, will the Father know his child?

To summarize this concept, I quote a verse from the hymn "God Loves Us So He Sent His Son."

> In word and deed he doth require
> My will to his, like son to sire,
> Be made to bend, and I, as son,
> Learn conduct from the Holy One.
> *(Hymns,* no. 187, verse 4)

Have You Experienced a Mighty Change of Heart?

Have you ever had a dream that you didn't remember until someone said something that jarred your memory? I dreamed I was in a room, and in front of me was a large door. It was slightly ajar. Light was beaming from around the edges of the door. I knew the Savior was on the other side of it, so I walked over and pushed the door shut. I did not remember anything of the dream until later that day. I was riding in a car with a man who said he wished we had more spiritual experiences in our life. When he said this, I remembered the dream and said, "We could have more; we are the ones who keep them out." In many instances we are the reason for the lack of contact with spiritual things.

John 7:17 tells us that we must do the Lord's will if we wish to know of the doctrine. We cannot live a life full of spiritual experiences while continuing to sin. We have to choose. From the beginning, God has given us agency (see Moses 4:3; 7:32), and when Christ fulfilled the Atonement, He took upon Himself the sins of all who would receive Him as their Savior. In doing so,

He felt all the effects of sin even though He was sinless. He felt pain as the soldiers nailed Him to the cross. He felt loneliness as He was left by His disciples. He felt burdened as He carried His own cross as far as He could. He felt humiliation as wicked men spat upon Him. He felt the consequences of sin while still remaining perfect.

But there was one effect of sin He had not felt before, and that was the loss of the Spirit. While He was on the cross, He said a phrase to His Father that is interpreted to mean, "My God, My God, why has thou forsaken me?" (Matthew 27:46). Can you understand what it must feel like to be perfect and yet lose the Spirit? Can you imagine the joy that comes to a sinner that regains the Spirit? We can't afford to live without it. We must do everything we can to maintain or regain the Spirit. This was made possible through the Savior's atonement.

I've tried to express my feelings about the Atonement in the following poem:

"Live as he Lives"

Oh consider in wonder how merciful He is,
to condescend to our level that we could rise to His.
He came to this world, though God from the start,
to take on infirmities, to succor man's heart.
His bowels filled with mercy, being tempted for all,
to loosen the bands of death from the fall.
He must be a mortal but death as He willed.
He has borne our griefs; with His stripes we are healed.
He made us free agents to act on our own;
All sins and their pains He bore all alone.
He paid the price, our Savior, our King
He requires from us this one vital thing.
This is the choice and consequence He gives:
Suffer as He suffered or live as He lives.

Doctrine and Covenants 19:16-18 says: "For behold, I, God, have suffered these things for all, that they might not suffer if they would repent; But if they would not repent they must suffer even as I; Which suffering caused myself even God, the greatest of all, to tremble because of pain, and to bleed at every pore, and to suffer both body and spirit. . . ."

Have you experienced a mighty change of heart and lost the desire for sin? Are you like your Father? Does the light of Christ shine in your eyes? Have you received His image in your countenance? Is there anything in your life that is interfering with spiritual guidance? If there is, change it.

Avoid the temptation to judge others, and always remember the Savior's need for us. It is my prayer that we may always stand as a witness for Him.

Chapter Nine

Heaven Means
So Much More

A few years ago I received a phone call from my sister-in-law in Idaho informing me that my mother was dying. She had been going down hill for a couple of years. She had a degenerating cerebellum, and now her language and motor skills were about gone. My mom, a social butterfly, had lost her ability to communicate. Out of all the physical problems she would eventually have, I think this one was the most difficult for her to endure.

As I entered the room where she was resting, I noticed there was no focus in her eyes. She was staring at the ceiling with no expression on her face. It broke my heart. Ever since I was a little boy, I loved to make my mom smile. I was the youngest of her seven children. If she were sad or mad at someone else in the family, I would do something silly to try to make her smile. But now as I spoke to her, rubbed her hand, and ran my fingers through her hair, I couldn't get a reaction. I wanted to talk with her. Finally, I resorted to putting my face within a few inches of hers—eye to eye. Then slowly I pulled away until at last, she focused on my eyes and a big smile appeared on her face. Nothing had ever felt so good. I said, "Mom, I love you." And in her best voice possible she replied, "I love you, too." Those were the last words I ever heard her say. But, oh, what wonderful words they were.

Throughout my life, nothing gave me more joy than making my mother smile. But somehow my parents were able to help me realize an even more glorious joy—that of making my Father in Heaven smile. Through my parents' love and nurturing, I began to have the desire to always live my life in such a way that my Heavenly Father could look at me, get a big smile on His face, and then say "I love you." Like Nephi of old, I was indeed born of goodly parents. For they gave me a taste of heaven.

But what about heaven? To many, it is a bizarre mix of Christianity and mythology, something so boring that those lucky enough to be allowed in, get to sit around and play the harp for eternity. But as Latter-day Saints, we know that we have been blessed with an opportunity to search for an understanding of heaven in the greatest revelation given to man. Melvin J. Ballard said, "The greatest revelation the Lord, Jesus Christ, has ever given man, so far as a record is made, was given to the Prophet Joseph Smith on the 16th of February 1832, known as *the 76th section* of the book of "Doctrine and Covenants" (Melvin J. Ballard, "The Three Degrees of Glory," pp. 3-4 / A Discourse at the Ogden Tabernacle, September 22, 1922; emphasis added).

Joseph Smith said, "Could you gaze into heaven five minutes, you would know more than you would by reading all that ever was written on the subject" (Joseph Smith, *History of the Church,* 6:50). Because the vision found in section 76 is literally a glimpse into heaven, it "gives more light, more truth, more principle than any revelation contained in any other book. . . ." (Wilford Woodruff, *Journal of Discourses* 22:146-147; hereafter referred to as *JD*).

In fact, when this vision came, the world had been so unaware of the truths of the plan of happiness that even Brigham Young had difficulty understanding this new light. He said:

> Many things which were revealed through Joseph came in contact with our own prejudices: We did not know how to understand them. . . . After all, my traditions were such, that when the Vision came first

to me, it was directly contrary and opposed to my former education. I said, Wait a little. I did not reject it; but I could not understand it. *(JD, 6:280-81)*

THE THEME

In the beginning of section seventy-six of the Doctrine and Covenants, there appears to be a statement of purpose for this divine revelation. Verse five reads, "For thus saith the Lord—I, the Lord, am merciful and gracious unto those who fear me, and delight to honor those who serve me in righteousness and in truth unto the end." It is gratifying to look for these principles of hope and mercy while reading this section. The Lord blesses and loves all flesh. He is definitely merciful to all His children, but the righteous are favored of God (see 1 Nephi 17:35). The vision is full of principles that show mercy to all and encouragement for righteousness in order to obtain the fullness of these blessings.

THE FEW THAT ARE LOST (SONS OF PERDITION)

Who are the Sons of Perdition? In this vision (Section 76), in verses 31-43, we read about seven reasons that some people become lost:

> Thus saith the Lord concerning all those who know my power, and have been made partakers thereof, and suffered themselves through the power of the devil to be overcome, and to deny the truth and defy my power. . . . Having denied the Holy Spirit after having received it . . . And saves all the works of his hands, except those sons of perdition who deny the Son after the Father has revealed him. (Emphasis added.)

In harmony with the vision, Joseph Smith said:

> All sins shall be forgiven, except the sin against the Holy Ghost; for Jesus will save all except the

sons of perdition. What must a man do to commit the unpardonable sin? He must receive the Holy Ghost, having the heavens opened unto him, and know God, and then, sin against Him. After a man has sinned against the Holy Ghost, there is no repentance for him. He has got to say that the sun does not shine while he sees it; he has got to deny Jesus Christ when the heavens have been opened unto him, and to deny the plan of salvation with his eyes open to the truth of it; and from that time he begins to be an enemy. *(Teachings of the Prophet Joseph Smith,* p. 358)

In the comparison chart given here, notice the correlation between the scriptures and the words of the prophet, Joseph Smith.

COMPARISON CHART
What must a man do to commit the unpardonable sin?
(See D&C 76:31,35,43, with *Teachings of the Prophet Joseph Smith,* p. 358.)

Know my power	Know God
Made partakers thereof	Have the heavens opened unto him.
Suffered themselves through the power of the devil to be overcome	Sin against Him
Deny the truth	Deny the plan of salvation with his eyes open to the truth of it
Defy my power	Say that the sun does not shine while he sees it

Denied the Holy Spirit after having received it	Receive the Holy Ghost
Deny the Son after the Father has revealed him	Deny Jesus Christ when the heavens have been opened unto him.

As to the fate of sons of perdition, it is enough to say, "Nevertheless, I, the Lord, show it by vision unto many, but straightway shut it up again; Wherefore, the end, the width, the height, the depth, and the misery thereof, they understand not, neither any man except those who are ordained unto this condemnation" (D&C 76:47-48). What a blessing—to never comprehend the destiny of the sons of perdition.

STEPS TO HEAVEN

One of the most enjoyable times to teach the gospel is at a baptism. New converts seem hungry for the gospel. They want to learn so much, yet they seem dazed with all that is happening. When I have been asked to give a talk in such situations, I like to teach the basics of the gospel with the convert participating. I will cut out five pieces of paper to look like big rocks. Then I will write on them *Faith, Repentance, Baptism, Confirmation,* and *Endure to the End* (see 2 Nephi 31:13-21). Then I will write their name on a sheet of paper and *Heaven* on another sheet of paper. I ask the person to stand on the paper where I've written his or her name, then I've placed the paper that says *heaven* on the floor across the room. I ask the individual if he or she can make it across the room without touching the floor in between. The answer is no, obviously. So I put down the other sheets as stepping stones, placing them face down. The individual can then go from one stepping stone to another until reaching *heaven*. Then I turn the stepping stones over to show what those steps are.

The scriptures teach us that no unclean thing can enter into the kingdom of heaven (see 1 Nephi 15:34). Our Father in

Heaven wants us to enter His kingdom so the Lord commanded us to be perfect (see Matthew 5:48, see Joseph Smith Translation). The word "perfection" implies more of a statement of completeness; not a declaration that we are without flaws. In fact, the Japanese word for *perfect* used in the scriptures seems to mean *completely whole.* "Be ye therefore perfect," becomes an invitation to become whole or complete. The Lord's command to be perfect appears to be more concerned with the completion of the journey than with the expectation of flawless travel throughout that journey.

To some members of the Church, our journey to perfection—or in other words, heaven—naturally seems impossible. But the Lord through His mercy has provided stepping stones for us that make this commandment attainable. Without the Lord we would inevitably express, "I can't be perfect, nobody's perfect." But with the Lord, all things are possible (see Luke 1:37). According to section seventy-six there appears to be a way provided. Regarding those who will enter the celestial kingdom, it says,

> They are they who *received the testimony of Jesus, and believed on his name* and were *baptized* after the manner of his burial, being buried in the water in his name, and this according to the commandment which he has given—
>
> That by keeping the commandments they might be washed and cleansed from all their sins, and receive the Holy Spirit by the laying on of the hands of him who is ordained and sealed unto this power;
>
> And who *overcome by faith,* and are *sealed by the Holy Spirit of promise* which the Father sheds forth upon all those who are just and true.

FIRST FOUR PRINCIPLES

The first four principles are in accordance with the Fourth Article of Faith. If we have participated in these four principles, including receiving the Holy Ghost, as we were told when confirmed, then we have a head start on our journey.

Overcoming

Of course, we aren't always found keeping the commandments. Therefore, we should persistently obey the command to repent. In Doctrine and Covenants 76:53, you probably noticed the phrase "overcome by faith." I was interested why it said "overcome" and not "overcame." Then, as I thought about the principles of hope and mercy, it became obvious to me. "Overcame" means we've already done it. "Overcome" means we *are* still doing it now. The voyage is not over. We are in the process, but we must endure to the end (see D&C 14:7). Even if it feels like you're losing, even if you feel like you've already lost, remember the Lord is on our side. With His help we can overcome all things by faith. Remember, to make a mistake is human, but to "overcome by faith" is heavenly (see Mosiah 3:19).

Made Perfect

Notice the compassionate words in verse sixty-nine: "These are they who are just men *made perfect* through Jesus the mediator of the new covenant, who wrought out this perfect atonement through the shedding of his own blood" (D&C 76:69; emphasis added). Let us be faithful in our battle against Satan until we, by our enduring faith in Christ and by His grace, eventually conquer. We must do all we can and then He will make up the difference (see 2 Nephi 25:23). He will reach our reaching (see *Hymns*, no. 129).

Sealed by the Holy Spirit of Promise.

As we righteously make progress toward the celestial kingdom, our actions are sealed by the Holy Spirit of Promise (D&C 76:53). This means that we have literally been approved by the Lord. Bruce R. McConkie wrote:

The Holy Spirit of Promise is the Holy Spirit promised the saints, or in other words the Holy Ghost. This name-title is used in connection with the sealing and ratifying power of the Holy Ghost, that is, the power given him to ratify and approve the righteous acts of men so that those acts will be binding on earth and in heaven. "All covenants, contracts, bonds, obligations, oaths, vows, performances, connections, associations, or expectations," must be sealed by the Holy Spirit of Promise, if they are to have "efficacy, virtue, or force in and after the resurrection from the dead; for all contracts that are not made unto this end have an end when men are dead." (D&C 132:7.)

To seal is to ratify, to justify, or to approve. Thus an act which is sealed by the Holy Spirit of Promise is one which is ratified by the Holy Ghost; it is one which is approved by the Lord; and the person who has taken the obligation upon himself is justified by the Spirit in the thing he has done. The ratifying seal of approval is put upon an act only if those entering the contract are worthy as a result of personal righteousness to receive the divine approbation. They "are sealed by the Holy Spirit of promise, which the Father sheds forth upon all those who are just and true." (D&C 76:53.) If they are not just and true and worthy the ratifying seal is withheld.(Bruce R. McConkie, *Mormon Doctrine*, pp. 361-362)

Melvin J. Ballard said, ". . . Even though men are able to deceive their brethren, they are not able to deceive the Holy Ghost . . ." (Melvin J. Ballard, "The Three Degrees of Glory," pp. 3-4 / A Discourse at the Ogden Tabernacle, September 22, 1922). Our progress on the way to heaven must be made in righteousness and truth. For no action is approved of the Lord unless it is sealed by the Holy Spirit of Promise.

One More Step

In Doctrine and Covenants section 131, verses 1-4, we learn of one more important step toward heaven. It reads:

> In the celestial glory there are three heavens or degrees;
> And in order to obtain the highest, a man must enter into this order of the priesthood [meaning the new and everlasting covenant of marriage];
> And if he does not, he cannot obtain it.
> He may enter into the other, but that is the end of his kingdom; he cannot have an increase.

I can't imagine heaven being heaven without this step. In other words, how could there be a heaven without my sweet wife. Without her I would not be whole. I would be incomplete. I am so thankful for the principle of mercy that seals me and my wife together for eternity—now that is heaven.

One of my favorite quotes that teaches hope for the forever family, was delivered by President Boyd K. Packer in general conference in 1992.

> It is not uncommon for responsible parents to lose one of their children, for a time, to influences over which they have no control. They agonize over rebellious sons or daughters. They are puzzled over why they are so helpless when they have tried so hard to do what they should. It is my conviction that those wicked influences one day will be overruled.
>
> "The Prophet Joseph Smith declared—and he never taught more comforting doctrine—that the eternal sealings of faithful parents and the divine promises made to them for valiant service in the

Cause of Truth, would save not only themselves, but likewise their posterity. Though some of the sheep may wander, the eye of the Shepherd is upon them, and sooner or later they will feel the tentacles of Divine Providence reaching out after them and drawing them back to the fold. Either in this life or the life to come, they will return. They will have to pay their debt to justice; they will suffer for their sins; and may tread a thorny path; but if it leads them at last, like the penitent Prodigal, to a loving and forgiving father's heart and home, the painful experience will not have been in vain. Pray for your careless and disobedient children; hold on to them with your faith. Hope on, trust on, till you see the salvation of God." (Orson F. Whitney, *Conference Report*, April 1929, p. 110)

We cannot overemphasize the value of temple marriage, the binding ties of the sealing ordinance, and the standards of worthiness required of them. When parents keep the covenants they have made at the altar of the temple, their children will be forever bound to them. President Brigham Young said:

"Let the father and mother, who are members of this Church and kingdom, take a righteous course, and strive with all their might never to do a wrong, but to do good all their lives; if they have one child or one hundred children, if they conduct themselves towards them as they should, binding them to the Lord by their faith and prayers. I care not where those children go, they are bound up to their parents by an everlasting tie, and no power of earth or hell can separate them from their parents in eternity; they will return again to the fountain from whence they sprang." (Joseph Fielding Smith Jr., *Doctrines of Salvation*, comp. Bruce R. McConkie, vol. 2, pp. 90-91.) (Boyd K. Packer, *Ensign*, May 1992, p. 68)

To the Latter-day Saint, heaven means so much more. It means that we can be with our families forever. Let us be faithful in obtaining the highest level of the celestial kingdom by entering into the new and everlasting covenant of marriage—sealing our families to us for time and all eternity.

WISHES AND WHIMS

When I ask a class, "What would you wish for if you had three wishes?" someone almost always says, "I would wish to go automatically to the celestial kingdom." The only problem is that if they're not prepared to be there, they would actually be sending themselves to hell. Elder Neal A. Maxwell said, "We cannot share in [God's] power without sharing in His attributes . . . we cannot reenter His house until our behavior would let us feel at home" (*Conference Report,* October 1986, pp. 69-73). When we share in God's attributes, when we are like Him, then it really does not matter where we are, we will be at home with Him. In fact, this can even happen while we still live in our mortal probation. "Indeed, he is then, even on earth, in the celestial kingdom of God" (John A. Widtsoe, *Evidences and Recollections,* p. 164).

But if we were not prepared to be with our Father in Heaven, and were placed in His presence, it would not be heaven. Brigham Young said, ". . . Forced into the presence of the Father and the Son . . . would be a hell to them" (*JD,* 8:153-54). He also said, "It would be no blessing to you to be carried into the celestial kingdom, and obliged to stay therein, unless you were prepared to dwell there" (*JD,* 3:221).

There is mercy in our eternal home. We will go to a degree of glory in which we feel at home. Our merciful God does not sentence a man to dwell in a higher state than he may actually deserve (see James E. Talmage, *Conference Report,* April 1930, pp. 94-98). When this life is over, we will continue our existence as the same person. President Spencer W. Kimball said, "Have you ever realized that there is no magic in death, that ceasing to breathe does not make angels of careless people, does not make believers of disbelievers, does not bring faith where there was skepticism?" (*The Teachings of Spencer W. Kimball*, p. 41). That is why the prophet Amulek said, "Ye cannot say, when ye are brought to that awful crisis, that I will repent, that I will return to my God. Nay, ye cannot say this; for that same spirit which doth possess your bodies at the time that ye go out of this life, that same spirit will have power to possess your body in that eternal world" (Alma 34:34).

The day will come that the disobedient will again be in the presence of God, and behold His face, and remain in their sins (see 2 Nephi 9:38). And in that awful state, "we shall not dare to look up to our God; and we would fain be glad if we could command the rocks and the mountains to fall upon us to hide us from his presence" (Alma 12:14). Can you imagine being compelled to remain in such a state? Moroni said it this way:

> Do ye suppose that ye shall dwell with him under a consciousness of your guilt? Do ye suppose that ye could be happy to dwell with that holy Being, when your souls are racked with a consciousness of guilt that ye have ever abused his laws?
>
> Behold, I say unto you that ye would be more miserable to dwell with a holy and just God, under a consciousness of your filthiness before him, than ye would to dwell with the damned souls in hell.
>
> For behold, when ye shall be brought to see your nakedness before God, and also the glory of God, and the holiness of Jesus Christ, it will kindle a flame of unquenchable fire upon you. (Mormon 9:3-5)

In the hypothetical situation of having three wishes, it would be better not to wish to go to the celestial kingdom, but rather to become a celestial person—a person whose thoughts, words, deeds and desires, in other words, whose heart is celestial (see Mosiah 4:30 and D&C 137:9).

Likewise, in our actual situation, it is still a matter of who we are that makes the difference. Or what we have become by the end of our journey. "No amount of testimony, no amount of knowledge, even knowledge that this is God's work will ever save a man . . . but the keeping of the commandments of God will entitle him to that blessing" (Heber J. Grant, *Conference Report,* October 1900, p. 59).

The Lord, in His mercy, will not allow everyone "that saith unto [him], Lord, Lord [to] enter the kingdom of heaven; but [they] who doeth the will of [his] Father which is in heaven" (Matthew 7:21). For those who do His will are prepared to dwell there. They must *become*—not just profess (see Titus 1:16).

IT'S A FULL CHANCE

If while searching for copper in a cave, you stumbled upon a room of copper, would you not carry out as much copper as you possibly could? But let's say that while hauling your massive load of copper, you noticed a room full of silver. Wouldn't you unload all of the copper and replace it with a fresh treasure of silver? And then, if while making your way out of the cave with your load of silver, you noticed a room full of gold, wouldn't you gladly leave behind the silver, and use every space possible to obtain and carry the gold? (See "The Tinder Box," *Harvard Classics*, Charles W. Eliot, New York: P. T. Collier and Son, 1909, vol. 17, pp. 349-50).

Just because we've already laid hold upon the lesser worldly treasures, that doesn't mean we've missed our chance for celestial progression. The celestial gold found in the gospel might not yet be in our view. Many people of this earth who have seen and obtained treasures of copper and silver would gladly give it up if they could find the treasure of the living gospel.

There is hope for individuals who have not yet heard the message. There is also hope for those who have not yet understood. President Harold B. Lee said, "We do not believe in the gospel of the second chance. We do not believe in the gospel of the first chance but we believe in a chance or full opportunity for everyone to hear and to accept the Gospel" (Harold B. Lee, *Conference Report,* April 1953, p. 25). We need to help others see the gold, and help them in their desire to obtain it.

I don't recall the exact details, but Sesame Street's Cookie Monster was given three options after he won a contest. He could have a cookie immediately, a sports car in a little while, or a mansion if he were willing to wait a little longer. It isn't difficult to figure out which one he chose. Sometimes people are like the Cookie Monster. Satan effectively influences people to trade forever for a brief moment.

As we help others obtain the blessings of heaven, we must also help them to retain their hope in those blessings. In sustaining our hope in a full chance, we should also remember the warnings of Elder Melvin J. Ballard, who taught, "Every man and woman who is putting off until the next life the task of correcting and overcoming the weakness of the flesh are sentencing themselves to years of bondage. . . ." (Melvin J. Ballard, *Three Degrees of Glory,* pp. 12-13).

Alma the Elder said:

> I beseech of you that ye do not procrastinate the day of your repentance until the end; for after this day of life, which is given us to prepare for eternity, behold, if we do not improve our time while in this life, then cometh the night of darkness wherein there can be no labor performed. (Alma 34:33)

BE VALIANT

We read in Doctrine and Covenants 76:79 that a person must be valiant in order to obtain the celestial kingdom. Those that are valiant persist in their battle to improve. Brigham Young said, "Those who are valiant and inspired with the true independence of heaven, [are they] who will go forth boldly in the service of their God, leaving others to do as they please, determined to do right, though all mankind besides should take the opposite course" (*JD* 1:312). Elder Bruce R. McConkie gave a wonderful discourse on the meaning of being valiant which I put in outline form to point out the main ideas more clearly.

To be valiant is:
    to come unto Christ
    to be perfected in Him
    to deny ourselves of all ungodliness
    to love God with our might, mind, and strength
    to believe with unshakable conviction
    to know the divinity of the Lord's work on earth
    to press forward with a steadfastness in Christ
    to have a perfect brightness of hope
    to love God and all men
    to endure to the end
    to live our religion
    to practice what we preach
    to keep the commandments
    to have the manifestation to pure religion
    to visit the fatherless and widows
    to keep ourselves unspotted before the world
    to bridal our passions
    to control our appetites
    to rise above carnal and evil things
    to overcome the world
    to be morally clean
    to pay our tithes and offerings
    to honor the Sabbath
    to pray with full purpose of heart
    to lay our all upon the altar

to take the Lord's side on every issue
to vote as He would vote
to think what He thinks
to believe what He believes
to say what He would say
to do what He would do in the same situation
to have the mind of Christ
to be one with Christ.
(Bruce R. McConkie, *Conference Report*, November, 1974)

Being valiant doesn't mean being perfect. Being valiant is an attitude or desire, a desire to change and improve. To desire to be like Christ. Notice the inspiring lyrics of the hymn, "More Holiness Give Me,"

> More holiness give me, More strivings within,
> More patience in suff'ring, More sorrow for sin,
> More faith in my Savior, More sense of his care,
> More joy in his service, More purpose in prayer.
>
> More gratitude give me, More trust in the Lord,
> More pride in his glory, More hope in his word,
> More tears for his sorrows, more pain at his grief,
> More meekness in trial, More praise for relief.
>
> More purity give me, More strength to o'ercome,
> More freedom from earth stains, More longing for home.
> More fit for the kingdom, More used would I be,
> More blessed and holy—More, Savior, like thee.
> ("More Holiness Give Me," *Hymns*, no. 131)

Listen to the words of hope and inspiration to be more valiant from our beloved Prophet, Gordon B. Hinckley:

> Each of us can do a little better than we have
> been doing. We can be a little more kind. We can

be a little more merciful. We can be a little more forgiving. We can put behind us our weaknesses of the past and go forth with new energy and increased resolution to improve the world about us, in our homes, in our places of employment, in our social activities.

We have work to do, you and I, so very much of it. Let us roll up our sleeves and get at it, with a new commitment, putting our trust in the Lord.

> Come, come, ye Saints, no toil nor labor fear;
> But with joy wend your way.
> Though hard to you this journey may appear,
> Grace shall be as your day.
> ("Come, Come, Ye Saints," *Hymns*, no. 30)

We can do it, if we will be prayerful and faithful. We can do better than we have ever done before.

The Church needs your strength. It needs your love and loyalty and devotion. It needs a little more of your time and energy. *(Conference Report*, April 1995, pp. 117-18; or *Ensign*, May 1995, p. 88)

BEYOND UNDERSTANDING

The purpose of man is clarified in 2 Nephi 2:25, where we read, "Adam fell that men might be; and men are, that they might have joy." What a great plan–we exist that we might have joy. Everyone (except the sons of perdition) will receive glory beyond understanding. In fact, according to John A. Widtsoe, "The meanest sinner, in the final judgement, will receive a glory which is beyond human understanding, which is so great that we are unable to describe it adequately. . . ." (*Message of the Doctrine and Covenants*, p. 167). Of course, in our Father's house are many mansions, and we will receive our inheritance according to our own works and through the grace of the Savior (see John 14:2 and D&C 76:111). All are degrees of glory. We just desire all that He wants us to have.

And thus we saw the glory of the celestial, which excels in all things—where God, even the Father, reigns upon his throne forever and ever; . . .

They who dwell in his presence are the church of the Firstborn; and they see as they are seen, and know as they are known, having received of his fulness and of his grace;

And he makes them equal in power, and in might, and in dominion. (D&C 76:92-95)

The Lord said, "For behold, this is my work and my glory—to bring to pass the immortality and eternal life of man" (Moses 1:39). With that in mind, it is no great wonder that Charles W. Penrose said, "While there is one soul of this race, willing and able to accept and obey the laws of redemption, no matter where or in what condition it may be found, Christ's work will be incomplete until that being is brought up from death and hell, and placed in a position of progress, upward and onward, in such glory as is possible for its enjoyment and the service of the great God" (*"Mormon" Doctrine* [Salt Lake City: George Q. Cannon and Sons, 1897], p. 72). May we partake in that glory. May we help others progress to that glory. And may we always find hope and mercy in that great plan of happiness.

CONCLUSION

Throughout my life, nothing gave me more joy than making my beloved mother smile. But nothing I could do would make her smile more than living my life in such a way that when the time came to stand before my Father in Heaven, He would smile. For this was her purpose and joy: That Heavenly Father would smile upon her children and bless them with eternal life. I look forward to that experience.

Elder Henry B. Eyring said, "When you see him, you will know his voice, because you will have prayed, listened, obeyed, and come to share the thoughts and intents of his heart" Then, quoting President Ezra Taft Benson, Elder Eyring continued, "Nothing is going to startle us more when we pass through the veil to the other side than to realize how well we know our Father and how familiar his face is to us" (*Ensign*, May 1991, p. 67).

It is my hope that as I see His familiar face, He will smile at me and with satisfaction in His eyes say, "Well done, thou good and faithful servant. . . . " (Matthew 25:21).

SELECTED BIBLIOGRAPHY

Benson, Ezra Taft, "In His Steps," 14-Stake Fireside, BYU, 4 March 1979. Printed in *1978-79 BYU Speeches of the Year*. Provo, Utah: BYU Press, pp. 59-65.

———. *Teachings of Ezra Taft Benson*. Salt Lake City: Bookcraft, 1988.

Brown, Hugh B. *Eternal Quest*. Salt Lake City: Bookcraft, 1956.

Cannon, George Q. *Gospel Truth*. Salt Lake City: Deseret Book, copyright 1957.

Evans, Richard L. *Thoughts for One Hundred Days*, Vol. 4. Salt Lake City: Publishers Press, 1970.

Grant, Heber J. *Gospel Standards*. Salt Lake City: Improvement Era, 1941, 1943.

Hymns of The Church of Jesus Christ of Latter Day Saints. Salt Lake City: Corporation of the President of the Church of Jesus Christ of Latter-day Saints, 1985

Kimball, Camilla. "Ye Are Free to Choose." In *Agency and the Latter-day Saint Woman*. Ed. Maren M. Mouritsen. Provo, Utah: Brigham Young University Press, 1981.

Kimball, Spencer W. *The Miracle of Forgiveness*. Salt Lake City: Deseret Book, 1969.

———. *Teachings of Spencer W. Kimball*. Salt Lake City: Bookcraft, 1982.

McKay, David O. *Gospel Ideals*. Salt Lake City: Improvement Era, 1953.

McConkie, Joseph Fielding. *The Spirit of Revelation*. Salt Lake City: Deseret Book, 1984.

Penrose, Charles W. *"Mormon" Doctrine*. Salt Lake City: George Q. Cannon and Sons, 1897.

Pinegar, Max L. "The Weightier Matters of the Law," *Speeches of the Year 1975*. 108-115.

Pratt, Parley P. *Key to the Science of Theology*. Salt Lake City: Deseret Book, 1978.

Smith, Joseph. *Teachings of the Prophet Joseph Smith.* Salt Lake City: Deseret Book, 1976.

Smith, Joseph F. *Gospel Doctrine.* Salt Lake City, Deseret Book, 1939.

Talmage, James E. *The Articles of Faith.* Salt Lake City, Deseret Book, 1988.

Teachings of the Latter-day Prophets. Church Educational System.

Wilford Woodruff: History of His Life And Labours, Ed. Matthias F. Cowley. Salt Lake City: Bookcraft, 1964.

Widtsoe, John A., *Evidences and Recollections.* Salt Lake City: Bookcraft, 1960.

——. *Message of the Doctrine and Covenants* Salt Lake City: Bookcraft, 1969.

Walton, Rick and Fern Oviatt, editors. *Stories for Mormons.* Salt Lake City, Bookcraft, 1983.

Journal of Discourses. Liverpool, R.D. and S. W Richards. 1854-1856.

ABOUT THE AUTHOR

Michael Weir Allred teaches seminary in the Ogden, Utah, area. He also teaches one religion class in Japanese at the Ogden Institute adjacent to Weber State University. In addition, he teaches for various CES programs, including Know Your Religion, Education Week, Especially for Youth, the Best of Especially for Youth, and Outreach Youth Conferences.

Brother Allred was born in Ogden, Utah, and went to Bonneville High School before serving a mission in Fukuoka, Japan. He graduated from Weber State University and later received a master's degree in counseling through the University of Phoenix. He spent seven years in the National Guard and Reserves, where he was trained in counter intelligence and was used as a Japanese interpreter.

His hobbies include playing the drums and working on his '67 Camaro. He loves to be with the youth, he loves to teach, he loves the gospel. He also loves sports and music, but most of all he loves his family. His wife, Kathy, was one of his best friends in high school. They now have four boys: Tyson, Joshua, Cody, and Kade.

Michael Weir Allred is a contributor in three of the Especially for Youth collections of published talks. He has also produced two talk tapes with Covenant Communications: *Get Ready, Get Set, Date!* and *You Might Be A Mormon If . . .*